HOW TO DO A SUPERIOR PERFORMANCE APPRAISAL

HOW TO DO A SUPERIOR PERFORMANCE APPRAISAL

William S. Swan, Ph.D.
with Phillip Margulies

JOHN WILEY & SONS, INC.

New York • Chichester • Brisbane • Toronto • Singapore

In recognition of the importance of preserving what has
been written, it is a policy of John Wiley & Sons, Inc., to
have books of enduring value published in the United
States printed on acid-free paper, and we exert our best
efforts to that end.

Copyright © 1991 by Swan Consultants, Inc.
Published by John Wiley & Sons, Inc.

Library of Congress Cataloging-in-Publication Data

Swan. William S.
    How To Do A Superior Performance Appraisal / by William Swan
  with Phillip Margulies.
      p.   cm.
    Includes index.
    ISBN 0-471-51469-1—ISBN 0-471-51468-3 (paper)
    1. Employees—Rating of.   I. Margulies, Phillip.   II. Title.
  HF5549.5.R3S8 1991
  658.3'125—dc20   90-46329
                                                             CIP

Printed in the United States of America

91 92 10 9 8 7 6 5 4 3 2

Preface: How To Use This Book

No two readers come to a book with exactly the same needs. With a "how-to" book this is especially true. You may know almost everything about the performance appraisal process, or next to nothing about it. You may read a lot of books on preparing a performance appraisal form for your department or division, or you may have just stepped into a job that, for the first time, gives you the responsibility for conducting performance appraisals. You may have a strong influence on your organization's performance appraisal program, or hardly any. Whatever your situation, there is something here for you. This preface will summarize and guide you quickly to the chapters you'll find the most helpful.

In Part I of this book I've tried to provide a context for everything that will come afterward: Chapter One, "Introduction: Why Managers and Employees Dread Performance Appraisals," examines some of the circumstances that, all too often, make the performance appraisal an event to be dreaded by manager and employee alike, and then goes on to suggest how it can be demystified for the employee and become a powerful tool for the manager. Chapter Two, "Performance Appraisal Systems," after briefly retracing the modern evolution of the performance appraisal and discussing some of its problems, takes each of the basic performance appraisal options in turn, explains their intentions and analyses, their weaknesses and strengths. This chapter is especially important in providing a "users" guide to *your* organization's performance appraisal program. You'll recognize your organization's performance appraisal program in any one of the methods that we'll review, or in some combination of them.

Chapter Three, "What Goes Wrong and Why" summarizes the problems of the performance appraisal, with especial attention to what can go wrong in the execution of the program.

Part II of the book presents a simple, easy-to-use approach to performance management that combines the best elements of the approaches that we surveyed in Part I. This is the approach I recommend if you have a choice. But even if you don't, I still recommend you read these chapters. They do more than present an overall approach to performance management. They cover techniques and principles that are useful even if you don't have the freedom to use my approach; later on, I'll show you how you can apply those techniques and principles to each of the approaches described in Chapter Two. Consider Part II as my vehicle for presenting universal tools of performance management as well as a particular performance management program.

Chapter Four, "The Swan Approach to Performance Management," gives a bird's eye view of my approach and explains why I think it combines the best features of the other programs.

Chapter Five, "Setting Good Performance Objectives," shows you how to make the most effective use of goal-setting appraisal techniques (both as used in my recommended program, and as it could be used in your organization).

Chapter Six, "Defining Performance Factors," puts into place a basic approach for evaluating *how* employees perform their work (the performance standards often referred to by phrases such as "quality of work," "motivation," "initiative," and so on).

Chapter Seven, "Creating an Employee Development Plan," sets forth a method for incorporating employee development into the appraisal itself.

Chapter Eight, "How To Make Your Organization's System Work." Often the manager must participate in an existing Performance Appraisal system in their organization. If that system departs from the ideal model presented in earlier chapters, this chapter shows how to incorporate effective strategies into that system and increase its effectiveness.

Chapter Nine, "Writing the Appraisal," shows how to rate performance and write the narrative portions of the appraisal.

Part III addresses in depth the aspect of the performance appraisal most dreaded by employees and managers alike: the face-to-face discussion of the appraisal, in which you let the employee know how he or she has been evaluated and set objectives or goals for the new appraisal period. Like any personal interaction, it's a complex and potentially unpredictable event. A great deal is at stake for both parties. When handled skillfully using the techniques I'll describe it can be the most rewarding part of the performance management process.

Chapter Ten, "Preparing for the Discussion and Building a Productive Atmosphere," shows you how to lay the groundwork so that both you and your employee come to the discussion with a good idea of what is to be accomplished and in the right frame of mind to accomplish it.

Chapter Eleven, "Structuring the Performance Appraisal Discussion," gives you a plan that will allow you to control and channel the meeting, and enable you to avoid drifting into digression or getting caught up on one issue.

Chapter Twelve, "Listening Skills," and Chapter Thirteen, "Questioning and Probing Techniques," provide communication skills and tools that you can apply to the basic structure of the performance appraisal discussion, and are also the skills used for ongoing coaching and counseling throughout the year.

Chapter Fourteen, "How to Cope with Defensiveness and Facilitate Problem Solving," scrutinizes these problems in detail and presents techniques for defusing and turning around emotions that are quite natural, but get in the way of productive communication.

Finally, Chapter Fifteen, "Conducting Fair and Legal Performance Appraisals," demystifies the confusing legal issues that often adversely affect the performance appraisal. The common sense guidelines I lay down here will give you the confidence to execute performance appraisals that are complete and accurate, as well as fair and legal.

Contents

HOW TO DO A SUPERIOR PERFORMANCE APPRAISAL

PART I

Background

CHAPTER ONE

Introduction: Why Managers and Employees Dread Performance Appraisals

The business climate has changed during the last ten years. It seems that no industry is immune to a shakeup as a direct or indirect consequence of deregulation or competition from abroad. For many organizations, one result of this trend is a justifiable obsession with quality and productivity. It's therefore more important than ever to accurately measure job performance so rewards can be distributed fairly and performance problems can be solved quickly.

A few decades ago the performance appraisal was a procedure of very limited utility, largely confined to hourly wage earners and used to pinpoint coarse distinctions between good and bad performers. Today many more job types and levels are subject to performance appraisals, and the performance appraisal is used for decisions about salaries, promotions and placement, to pinpoint performance problems, improve employee performance, for career counseling, and to help implement the strategies and instill the values of the organization. While some may question the wisdom of burdening the performance appraisal with *all* those objectives, almost no one seriously doubts the necessity for some system of evaluating employee performance. Yet, while conceding its importance, few employees or managers actually look forward to a performance appraisal.

You might say, "Well of course; few people look forward to a dental appointment, either. But it's a regrettable necessity, and most of us accept that fact." In the case of a dental appointment, however, at least the dentist is comfortable with his or her job, whereas a performance appraisal is often equally distasteful for manager and employee alike.

WHY EMPLOYEES DREAD PERFORMANCE APPRAISALS

For employees receiving performance appraisals, feelings of dread are easy to understand: they're being judged, after all. Employees know well in advance *when* judgment will be pronounced, but often have a much vaguer idea of what standards they're being judged by and how you, as a manager, think they measure up to them. Among those who know their performance has been shaky, the dread may be more acute, but even star performers have their misgivings: Suppose the appraisal doesn't take account of their perception of their true worth? They'd better be prepared to defend themselves, if they don't want to be done out of that raise.

From a practical standpoint, many things hang in the balance: salary, promotions, and perhaps the specific responsibilities that will be expected of them in the future.

The performance appraisal is also one of the most

emotionally charged procedures in management. People have very strong feelings about being evaluated. Employees can feel vulnerable at this point. If their work hasn't been satisfactory, now is when the boom will fall. If they're personally pleased with what they've accomplished during the appraisal period, they may know from experience that their idea of good performance may be completely at odds with their manager's and they may be due for a rude awakening. Who knows what insidious little checkmarks are being made on forms that will go into their permanent record, informing any future manager that they " lack initiative" and "have difficulty facing that fact" about themselves. Employees may try to dispute the assessment, but they know their word carries much less weight than their boss' supposedly expert opinion. The process may seem completely irrational to them but they don't have much to say about it.

No wonder employees who are comfortable in their jobs most of the year can feel like victims of authority, whether in the form of an arbitrary manager or due to the abstract expectations of the organization, as performance appraisal time approaches.

WHY MANAGERS DREAD THE PERFORMANCE APPRAISAL

Ironically, the manager, who is beginning to loom so large in the employee's consciousness as the day of reckoning nears, usually feels no better about the performance appraisal. Managers can list even more reasons for their lack of enthusiasm. Most of us don't like to sit in judgment of other people. It's that much worse if by doing so you risk offending someone whose continuing enthusiastic cooperation is a necessity for your own success. Your employees' performance is partly their responsibility and partly yours; but in most performance appraisal programs the *appraisal*—its fairness, accuracy, and effect on future productivity and employee morale—are entirely the responsibility of the employee's immediate supervisor. What if what you believe is an accurate appraisal leads to an Equal Employment Opportunity complaint? Can you be sure of avoiding that, even if you believe you are doing everything right? How can you really be fair and objective anyway, when the tasks the employee performs are so hard to measure, when it's so hard to separate one employee's contribution from the overall team effort? So much seems to fall on the shoulders of the manager doing the performance appraisal; it's no wonder that many managers do not relish the task.

In addition to all these reasons for lack of managerial enthusiasm there is another factor that the employee is probably unaware of, but of which the manager is very conscious: in most cases managers are not in a position to choose the system that's going to be used in the performance appraisal. In most cases managers have had little or no input into the development of either the form or the procedures. In large organizations this is understandable, and probably inevitable. After all, one of the purposes of the performance appraisal is to provide comparable data across all employees in a given role; in the interests of fairness the standards used to measure each employee should be the same—and chances are they would not be the same if each manager had the option of using his own appraisal system. But for whatever reasons, the performance appraisal, which is almost always the manager's sole responsibility, is generally handed down from on high like the Ten Commandments. The performance appraisal form and system may come down quietly, accompanied by a simple memo, or it may arrive with a great deal of pomp and formality. The form and procedures may be the product of a day's work, or they may be the final result of years of planning by human resource professionals. Perhaps it's no mere form or collection of forms; perhaps it's a carefully engineered *system*—some of the things it does are very basic; others are subtle. In some organizations the performance appraisal is the linchpin for an organization's human resource programs, including salary administration, human resource planning, and career pathing. Of all human resource programs, the performance appraisal may even be the only formal mechanism for communicating to employees what their job is. And, increasingly, the performance appraisal is used as legal documentation for validating promotion decisions.

It may seem as if, at a certain stage of development, someone has said, "as long as we're doing it— why not add *this*?" and tacked it on. As we'll see, the purposes for which performance appraisals are used have expanded gradually for many reasons, none of them whimsical, but whatever the motive, the result is the same: an increased burden on the manager who has to conduct the appraisal.

It's easy for managers to be cynical about performance appraisal. Often there's a poor match between the performance appraisal system and reality. Performance appraisal systems may ask managers to evaluate employees with whom they have little direct contact during the year—where is the manager supposed to get the data? Then again, the qualities the form measures may not seem to have much to do with the job the employee is asked to do. In some cases, managers may be aware that the system of measurement the performance appraisal uses is outmoded or invalidated by the research on the performance appraisal.

Finally, some managers ask, if the performance appraisal is so important, why aren't we given more support in conducting them? According to surveys conducted by Swan Consultants, Inc., only 25% of managers who do performance appraisals receive training for it. When there is training it often goes little further than to explain how to use the form, administrative procedures, and deadlines for submitting and getting the forms approved.

There's an inevitable temptation to give up making the performance appraisal work in reality, since the organization seems satisfied with what works only on paper. Why not glide through it, fill the forms out with a minimal effort, and talk about it with the employee in the easiest way. Surveys show that in some companies employees are not even aware of the existence of formal performance appraisal programs—they are surprised to learn that that once-a-year informal chat with the boss had anything to do with a formal review of their performance. The managers administering those programs are just going through the motions. But managers who do this are selling themselves short, because the performance appraisal can be a powerful *management* tool, and of all the parties involved, the managers are the ones it can benefit the most.

The most intractable problems of performance appraisals are those that affect the human resources function. To make the best and fairest placement and salary administration decisions, human resource programs require accurate, comparable data concerning every employee in the organization. That's a difficult goal to achieve. It can probably be accomplished only by instituting the most effective available performance appraisal methods and by giving thorough training and support to all managers conducting performance appraisals.

On the other hand, surveys show that managers are more interested in the other possible benefits of effective performance appraisals—benefits such as improving individual performance, making decisions about who needs training, and giving employee feedback. And fortunately, achievement of these objectives is well within your power as an individual, whatever performance appraisal system your organization uses.

Performance management, when considered as an ongoing *year-long* process of setting goals and objectives and giving ongoing coaching and feedback, can be an important vehicle for the individual manager's success. The performance appraisal is the annual codification of this ongoing process. It can be the means by which managers hold the reins of their department in their hands, monitor progress so that when something goes wrong you *know* it is, and can make mid-course changes while they're relatively easy to make, build and sustain good relationships with employees, and encourages team development among their employees. Managers who know how to make the best use out of whatever performance appraisal system their organization requires of them are more effective managers.

Perhaps your performance appraisal system seems to have arrived on your desk like a sophisticated software package without an instruction manual or user's guide, and with no hope of obtaining one. What can you do in a situation like that? Eventually, by trial and error, you'll learn how to run the software, because you have to. But you're probably not going to get it to do most of the really sophisticated things it can do—chances are, you won't even *know* about most of the things it can do. You'll probably realize only a small percentage of its potential. And when something goes wrong, you'll really be at a loss. You won't know what went wrong or how to fix it. That's the need this book was written to fill. If your performance appraisal system seems like software without a manual, you can look on this book as that missing manual: you may be pleasantly surprised to find that your performance appraisal system has features that can work for you. If your organization's performance appraisal system seems like the wrong tool for the job, and you have some say in the matter, this book can supply you with the logical arguments for changing it. If you're dissatisfied with your organization's performance appraisal program, but changing it isn't within your power, we'll suggest ways of reinterpreting it that can make it effective without straying from the strict letter of your organization's policies and procedures.

We can't guarantee that once you've absorbed the lessons herein some problems won't remain. You'll still be sitting in judgment of your employees, and you'll still be responsible for some tough decisions. The task of telling an employee when he or she is not performing up to standard is still a difficult one, even when you use the techniques for defusing defensiveness described later in this book. In short, this book can't promise to make the performance appraisal guaranteed fun, but it can put you on the road to making the performance appraisal work for you. It can help you stop looking on the performance appraisal as an unpleasant chore, and begin to regard it as a practical and versatile management tool. It can help you take whatever performance appraisal system your organization asks you to administer, and use it to fulfill your goals, the goals of the organization, and the goals of your employees.

PERFORMANCE MANAGEMENT VS. PERFORMANCE APPRAISAL

If there's one point I'd like you take from the pages ahead, it's the superior value of continuous *perfor-*

mance management in comparison with a once-a-year *performance appraisal*; or, to put it another way, the value of integrating the performance appraisal into a larger performance management process.

Performance management means more than assessing an employee's performance at regular intervals. It unites a number of related tasks: monitoring, coaching, giving feedback, gathering information, and yes, assessing an employee's work. It accomplishes those tasks in the context of objectives—the immediate objectives of the department and the overall goals of the organization. And it carries them out systematically, throughout the year.

For different organizations the actual means may differ, but regardless of the procedures used to implement it, the basic strategy is the same and the benefits are the same. A performance management approach makes better *use* of the performance appraisal, because it uses the information and the performance appraisal interaction to support definite goals; it also makes for a fairer and more accurate performance appraisal, because defining the aims of the organization and the department clearly helps form better, more job-related criteria for the appraisal.

PERFORMANCE MANAGEMENT AND THE BUSINESS STRATEGIES OF THE ORGANIZATION

Many organizations have enunciated mission statements, business strategies, core values, or driving forces that top management would like to communicate to its employees. Management would also like to have line managers, supervisors, and employees bring their principles to life by incorporating them into their everyday activities on the job.

It's a good idea, but all too often these bold statements of principle and purpose remain on wall plaques or paper at corporate headquarters. Well-executed performance management systems can cascade those strategies, values, and intentions down through the organizational hierarchy, so that each employee knows what they are and knows how his or her tasks, objectives, or responsibilities fit into the big picture.

A good performance management system will also help clarify the organization's core values or intentions. This may include ideals such as quality, customer service, positive interpersonal communication among staff, contribution to profitability, or ethical behavior. These ideals, if clearly stated and effectively communicated through a powerful performance management system, can be very helpful in guiding an individual employee in the course of his or her daily work. This process also makes clear that each employee is accountable for *how* things are done as well as *what* is done.

PERFORMANCE MANAGEMENT AND CAREER DEVELOPMENT

Whether you wish to improve an employee's skills and competencies in a current job, or facilitate succession planning or career planning, an effective performance management process can be quite helpful. In fact, most sophisticated performance appraisal forms have a separate section in which the implications of other sections are extracted and used to create a formal development plan. This can be used to develop employees in their current jobs, prepare them for other responsibilities or promotion, or at least provide a plan to enrich their experience in their current role.

By setting clear objectives, the performance management process lets employees know what is expected of them, what they need to do to meet those objectives, and the consequences of meeting, exceeding, or failing to meet them. For employees, being clear about what is expected of them and how they will be evaluated is often a positive experience.

A performance management system also helps the employee plan for future performance, since it sets clear targets and goals, and explains why those targets and goals may not have been achieved in the past. In addition, the performance management process can also provide a clear mechanism by which employees can be given developmental opportunities in their current job that will prepare them for promotion or advancement when such opportunity arises. The inclusion of a development plan in the performance appraisal process, rather than just focusing on a report card of last year's performance, gives employees a sense of *their* influence on *their* future.

How you'll make that all happen is the burden of this book.

As mentioned earlier, this book addresses itself to the reality of the performance appraisal as it is presently practiced. In other words, we're not just going to present an ideal performance management system for an ideal world; we're going to help you work with what you've got. What you've got may not lend itself to performance management as I've just described it. But even if the particular performance appraisal program you're working with makes it hard for you to act formally on our advice, there are ways you can do it in an informal way, and in later chapters I'll supply detailed suggestions as to how.

CHAPTER TWO

Performance Appraisal Systems

The seven most commonly used performance appraisal methods are described and analyzed in this chapter. Chances are that in one, or some combination, of these methods you'll recognize the approach you are required to use in appraising your employees. I will explain the logic and intention behind each approach, how it is supposed to work, what it's supposed to accomplish, and how its effectiveness is rated by researchers.

If you feel you understand the logic already, you can skip this chapter or just read the part about your performance appraisal system. However, you may find it worthwhile to read the whole chapter to see where your performance appraisal system fits into the overall picture; comparing your system to the others may even help you to understand why it was picked over the alternatives.

Before we take the performance appraisal approaches one by one, I'd like to set the stage with a brief discussion of the evolution of the performance appraisal. By showing the progression, I hope to give you a clearer idea of the issues and controversies addressed by the methods described in this chapter.

HISTORICAL BACKGROUND AND RECENT TRENDS

"The Imperial Rater of Nine Grades seldom rates men according to their merits, but always according to his likes and dislikes," the Chinese philosopher Sin Yu remarked around 1,700 years ago. We can draw a number of inferences from this quotation. For one thing, it's clear that not only has the performance appraisal been around a long time, but so have complaints about its fairness and accuracy. Secondly we can deduce—and more recent history confirms this judgment—that while new techniques of performance appraisal have been developed over the years, they have never displaced more traditional techniques. Too often we are still ranking and rating like the Imperial Rater of the Wei dynasty.

As we'll see, the introduction of modern performance systems such as management by objectives (MBO) and evaluation approaches such as behaviorally anchored rating scales (BARS), has not prevented many organizations from continuing to rely on old methods such as essay forms, peer ranking, and "trait" rating scales. In fact, sometimes a technique that goes back to the third century and the latest brainstorm of management theorists can be found side by side on the same form.

Widespread systematic use of performance appraisals in the United States began early in this century with the government and the military, where pressures for merit systems of promotion have traditionally created a demand for an objective measurement of performance. The modern versions of techniques such as peer ranking, forced-choice measures, and trait-rating scales were developed in the armed services. In civilian life, performance appraisals were used, but limited to hourly industrial employees after World War I; appraisal of managerial employees did not become popular until after World War II.

By the early 1950s most large organizations in this country had performance appraisal programs. For the most part, however, these programs were not very sophisticated. Managers simply rated employees "excellent," "good," "fair," or "unsatisfactory" on a series of traits such as "motivation" or "initiative." Top management was exempt from performance appraisal; at the most, the lower levels of management were included. Too often personnel decisions had very little to do with the appraisal. With some regularity, highly rated employees were fired and low-rated employees retained.

All this was changed dramatically by the 1964 Civil Rights Act and the 1966 and 1970 Equal Employment Opportunity Commission (EEOC) Guidelines for the regulation of employment selection procedures. By defining the performance appraisal as a "selection procedure," the guidelines made it a legal necessity for corporations to find more objective, more systematic, and above all, more defensible techniques for evaluating their employees.

Even before the civil rights legislation of the 1960s, management theorists like Peter Drucker (who developed the concept behind management by objectives, later applied to the performance appraisal) and large corporations such as RCA, General Motors, and Black and Decker had attempted to devise more objective and accurate performance appraisal techniques. Their discoveries began to be applied much more widely with the advent of civil rights legislation.

In essence, Equal Employment Opportunity Commission guidelines require that any test or selection device showing adverse impact be validated or proven relevant to job performance. These rules are applied to performance appraisals because appraisals are often used as an internal selection or promotion device. Some experts argue that the EEOC guidelines merely speeded up an already existing trend toward more accurate and sophisticated performance appraisals.

CRITERIA FOR RATING PERFORMANCE APPRAISAL METHODS

What constitutes a "good" performance appraisal technique? Researchers who looked into the performance appraisal process ask a series of questions about each method.

1. Is the information measured by the performance appraisal job relevant? If so, how accurate is the technique at measuring them?
2. Does the technique provide a fair and accurate basis for comparing different individuals with the same job in different parts of the organization?
3. Is the technique reliable—that is, will two different rating managers reach the same conclusion, all else being equal?
4. Is the performance information gathered useful and for what is it useful?

I'll be paying especially close attention in this chapter to that last question.

For practical purposes, what constitutes a good performance appraisal technique depends on what you want it to do. No performance appraisal method is perfect; each one represents a compromise between strengths and limitations. When researchers rate the rating systems, some score highest on legal defensibility, others are particularly well-adapted to giving feedback and improving employees' job performance, and others are best for purposes of internal transfer and salary administration. Even though there are some techniques that most researchers consider virtually useless, there are no techniques they consider effective for every purpose.

METHOD 1: GLOBAL ESSAYS AND RATINGS

This technique consists of just what its name suggests. At the end of the year (or whatever the chosen performance period is) the rating manager is handed a form consisting of the question: "What is your overall evaluation of this individual's performance for the past year?" On a series of blank lines provided for comment the manager then proceeds to exercise his or her talents for literary composition. Depending on that individual's inclination skills in that area, he or she may or may not welcome the opportunity.

The manager is allowed to write anything and to justify the evaluation by using examples, perhaps, or just gut feelings. Nothing on the form forces the manager to back up the judgment or suggests what criteria to use for making a decision. The manager and only the manager decides what data, if any, are relevant to the appraisal.

In a variation of this approach, there is no essay, just the rating: "outstanding," "excellent," "good," "fair," or alternately "superior," "more than satisfactory," "satisfactory," "less than satisfactory," and "poor."

It's hard to find anything to say in defense of global

rating methods of performance appraisal, whether in essay or simple grade-giving form, except that they harken back to an earlier and simpler time in the history of management. With respect to the EEOC guidelines, global essay performance appraisals are legally indefensible because they are not easily shown to be job related. Their accuracy as well as their fairness is questionable, because the same standard cannot be applied throughout the organization; each manager has his or her own criteria, and even the individual manager is likely to apply different criteria to individuals with the same job.

Not only the employee, but the organization, too, suffers from the inaccuracy of this method. The failure to break down the essay, at least in a regular standardized way, into dimensions or components of performance, severely limits its usefulness for placement purposes. The Human Resources Department may have the manager's word that a given individual is "an outstanding performer." But not knowing how or why this is the case, it's impossible to know whether that means the employee is qualified for any other job than the one he or she is already doing. Even if the essayist has volunteered that the employee's exceptional worth is based on "motivation" and "willingness to work hard," there's no basis for assuming that this employee is better motivated or more hardworking than another employee whose supervisor also called "outstanding" but happened not to adduce "motivation" and "willingness to work hard" as components of the assessment.

Finally, the essay form offers a poor foundation for the manager's goals of giving feedback, coaching, counseling and motivating employees, because it is unconvincing and arbitrary. If the employee objects to the appraisal you, as manager, can't say, "Well this is the standard, and other employees in your position are meeting it," because it's not true: There is no standard—just your opinion, and the employee realizes it.

METHOD 2: TRAIT RATING

Trait rating, in the form that follows, remains one of the most commonly used performance appraisal methods today. The centerpiece of the appraisal is a list of personality traits or qualities such as problem solving ability, cooperation, motivation, adaptability, innovativeness, among others. The rating manager assigns a number to each trait, indicating the degree to which the employee possesses that quality. A variation of this technique requires the manager to evaluate an employee on each of several trait labels, with brief definitions, along a line containing a variety of adjectives.

Typically, the organization that plans to use trait-rating scales first conducts a certain amount of informal analysis to determine what personality traits belong on the form. The problem is that, in most of the trait-rating scales currently in use, the traits are very broadly defined, and so are the criteria for determining the levels associated with each trait—that is, the basis for deciding whether someone is very motivated, slightly motivated, or not at all motivated are not clearly defined.

Trait-rating scales have much more to recommend them than the global essay approach, and the performance appraisal method I described in Chapters Five through Seven includes a variation of this technique. However, my suggested version of trait rating differs in crucial respects in the way the traits (which I call "performance factors") are generated and how they are used in the appraisal.

As currently practiced, trait rating is a flawed

procedure. Trait-rating scales have trouble standing up to the scrutiny of the courts because it is difficult to prove their job relevance. Without specific, job-relevant definitions, trait-rating scales are vulnerable to the errors associated with the subjective elements in an appraisal—errors such as the "halo effect," "strictness," "positive or negative leniency," "central tendency," and others. (For a more detailed discussion of these and other common errors see Chapter Three, "Common Rater Errors.")

Finally and most significantly for the rating manager, scales that rate individuals based on personality traits make a poor tool for employee development. If the manager seems to be rating employees on what they *are* rather than what they *do*, he or she is on shaky ground when asking employees to change. Imagine the rating manager saying to an employee: "You have to become more self-motivated if you want to get a better rating." The employee may think (even if he or she doesn't come out and say it): "Oh really? Who are you, my therapist?"

It's much more effective to tell an employee, "You're *acting* in this (clearly defined) way, and here are the consequences for you and us if this behavior continues. Let's try to find a way to modify it so you can be more effective." That gives the employee something to work on, something which has a limit and which is in the employee's power to change.

Trait-rating scales remain popular in the face of criticism by industrial psychologists because they address a real problem that other, more objective performance appraisal approaches do not address. Undoubtedly it would be more objective if we could base our judgment of employees' performance solely on their accomplishments. However the collective nature of most types of work makes it difficult to link a given employee with a given accomplishment.

Most people work in teams and even though the rating manager may have a gut feeling about who was the most valuable member of the team, he or she may find it very hard to measure that value objectively. Therefore it's necessary for the manager to make a general determination about what kind of daily behavior is required by the job.

Even in jobs such as sales, where an individual's performance can be isolated rating managers are usually concerned with *how* their employees go about accomplishing their goals. They don't want their salespeople gathering accounts through unethical practices (to use an extreme example) or making promises they can't keep (to use a more common one) just to meet prescribed performance levels.

Trait-rating scales are an attempt to take into account this on-going behavioral aspect of performance.

METHOD 3: PEER RANKING

Peer-ranking procedures were first developed by the armed services and are still in common use there. They are also familiar to most of us from school (remember class ranking?). Typically the form asks the rating manager to provide an overall evaluation of performance by checking one of the following categories: top 1%, top 3%, top 5%, top 10%, top 30%, top 50% (typical), bottom 30% (marginal), and unsatisfactory. As opposed to other ranking procedures, managers are asked to rank their employees with respect to other employees.

Peer-ranking procedures are not widely used outside the military, and they're seldom used by themselves. They generally comprise a line or two in an appraisal form. This makes good sense in that these procedures are really not a way of arriving at a judgment about an employee, only a way of expressing the judgment. Why and how this employee is better or worse than the average employee has to be supported and expressed by other means.

By the same token, ranking procedures are no more objective than the means used to support them. In a school, a computer uses test scores to determine mathematically in what percentile a given student belongs. There's very rarely that kind of input available regarding job performance.

In that case, why use peer-ranking procedures at all? Ranking procedures have the virtue of avoiding some of the common errors of subjective appraisal, such as "central tendency," "strictness," and "positive or negative leniency," because they force the rating manager to think of an entire group of employees and compare them to each other; certainly the manager is not going to put all employees in the center. However, in a large organization the process fails because the rating manager can't be familiar enough with the work of every employee in the organization to make a valid assessment. As a rule, ranking is not based on well-defined, job-relevant measures of performance and so will not stand up well in court. Even if the ranking is based on job-relevant measures, it's still difficult to back up the assertion that the manager knows the comparative worth of every employee, let alone how well they stack up against every other employee in the organization who has a similar job.

Ranking procedures may help the rating manager think about performance—in that comparing different workers can give an idea of what may reasonably be expected of the average worker; however, as an appraisal technique, they are not very useful because they are unrelated to the intention of the performance appraisal. In order to know how two workers rate against each other, the manager must know how they each rate against an independent standard; therefore he or she will still need some other appraisal method to arrive at that judgment.

METHOD 4: ORGANIZATIONAL RECORDS

At the opposite end of the spectrum from the free-form essay lies the performance appraisal based entirely on "hard" data which the organization regularly collects for purposes other than performance measurement. Such information might include accident and absence rates, production rates, cost variances, and most commonly, sales figures.

While organizational records like this can, in some instances, provide a highly objective and job relevant basis for measurement of performance, there are very few jobs to which this method can be applied effectively. For one thing, most objective data comes from measures of group performance rather than individual performance. Even where the individual contribution can be isolated, the abstract nature of the information limits its usefulness for the manager who wishes to provide feedback and help improve employees' job performance.

The relevance of the hard data represented by organizational records will vary dramatically with the individual job. Some jobs will lend themselves to this approach; others will not. When objective data gathered for purposes other than appraisal are useful, their effectiveness will probably lie in the support they lend to other appraisal techniques.

METHOD 5: CRITICAL INCIDENTS

The critical-incident method was developed in the 1950s specifically as an answer to flaws in the trait-

rating approaches already described. Where trait-
rating scales address themselves to the personality
of the employee, the critical-incident method is concerned purely with the facts of the employee's performance. Throughout the year the rating manager
documents the employee's positive and negative behaviors on the job. At the end of the year these
"critical incidents" are collected and compared: we
have two piles of evidence, and we are asking, essentially, which pile is higher.

The critical incident method is almost never used
by itself, and its value depends entirely on the larger
interpretive context in which it is employed. Its use
places a great deal of emphasis on observation and
documentation, and that is a potentially valuable feature of the method. However, the degree of "objec-
tivity" this emphasis implies can vary greatly, depending on who is doing the appraisal and what
standard is used for determining the relevance of a
given event. What constitutes a "critical incident?"
When you've collected a group of critical incidents,
what do they imply? Both of these questions leave
open large areas of interpretation that must be filled
by other appraisal techniques and procedures.

For the purposes of EEOC defensibility, it's certainly better to have documentation of an employee's
performance than not have it, but interpretation is
needed to show job relevance and fair comparison
with other employees. For placement purposes, the
critical incident is not very helpful unless it is used
to determine something more than whether an employee has more positive than negative behaviors.
Obviously, placement requires more subtle information. On the other hand, if the interpretive matrix
around the critical incidents (that is, the *other* performance appraisal techniques used in conjunction
with it) enables the rating manager to use the critical

incidents as supporting evidence for more subtle judgments, the technique can be more useful.

METHOD 6: BEHAVIORALLY BASED SCALES AND BEHAVIORALLY ANCHORED RATING SCALES (BARS)

The most elaborate, systematic and "scientific" of performance appraisal rating techniques are the behaviorally based scales and behaviorally anchored rating scales (BARS). BARS systems are expensive to initiate because (when done properly) they are based on a rigorous and lengthy analysis of each job to which the system will be applied.

The BARS scale used for a given job is arrived at by a 5-step process.

1. *Critical Incidents*—Individuals with detailed, first-hand knowledge of the job (such as incumbents and supervisors) list specific examples of effective and ineffective behavior.
2. *Performance Dimensions*—The collection of specific incidents arrived at in Step 1 are generalized into a set of "performance dimensions."
3. *Retranslation*—A second group of job-knowledgeable individuals is used to validate and refine the product of the first two steps. They are shown the original collection of incidents and asked to assign each incident to the dimension that best describes it. Those incidents that meet a predetermined percentage of agreement with the group in Step 2 are considered to be "retranslated" and are used in the BARS scale.
4. *Scaling Incidents*—The Step 3 group rates the behavior described in each incident in terms of ineffectiveness or effectiveness, using a 7- or 9-point scale.

5. *Final Instrument*—The retranslated scaled incidents are used as the "behavioral anchor" in à
   BARS instrument, which is comprised of a series
   of vertical scales (one per "performance dimension") that are anchored by the included incidents. Each incident is placed on the scales based
   on the rating determined in Step 4.

The strength of BARS lies in its creation of measures which are closely job-relevant. The systematic
background of the system, together with the job-
relevance of the behaviors it measures, make personnel decisions based on BARS information highly
defensible against EEOC suits.

BARS is preferred by industrial psychologists to
trait-rating scales, perhaps because it embodies very
sophisticated measuring procedures. It is all the more
surprising, then, that research has failed to prove
BARS more accurate than trait-rating scales. No
one knows for certain why BARS have not been
more successful, but the following factors undoubtedly contribute to the problem.

1. The accuracy of any given BARS system is de-
   pendent on the thoroughness of the initial, 5-step
   job analysis, and not every organization conducts
   the job analysis as scrupulously as it needs to.
   Needless to say, one organization can't use another's BARS; they must be willing to invest the
   time and effort to create their own instrument.
2. To apply BARS, managers must pay close attention and collect a great deal of data. The nature
   of the relationship between manager and employee may not make this a realistic possibility.
3. After all the investment in setting up BARS, many
   organizations fail to support the system by training managers in its use. After all, the managers
   are being asked to conduct careful behavioral ob-

servations and ratings. For assessment centers, the rater training is quite rigorous or professional raters, often psychologists, are used.

Thus BARS can be given a high rating on legal defensibility and a mixed rating on accuracy. As for the manager-employee goals of feedback, coaching, counseling, and improvement of job performance, BARS is good in that it gives manager and employee very specific things to talk about, but weak in that it is not goal-oriented.

METHOD 7: OBJECTIVES AND GOAL-SETTING PROCEDURES

Goal-setting procedures—sometimes called "management by objectives" or "work planning and review"—work by comparing expected performance with actual performance. At the beginning of the appraisal period, the manager, either alone or in collaboration with the employee, sets objectives or goals with standards or levels of accomplishment expected for set, interim periods. At the end of the appraisal period the employee is evaluated based on whether the goals were met and whether they were accomplished in accordance with the standards set at the beginning of the appraisal period.

Performance appraisal methods that work by setting specific goals and standards are strong in the areas where methods such as BARS and trait-rating scales are weak. They are objective (a goal was either met or not) and flexible (a different set of goals are worked out for each appraisal period and may be modified during the period), and highly relevant to the needs of the organization and of the manager doing the appraisal. They're work oriented and feedback oriented: the employee and the manager getting together and planning the year's work and the employee's expected part in it.

Of course, goal-setting procedures are weak where trait rating and BARS are strong. For jobs in which the actions performed by the employee are the same every day, period-long goals may not mean very much. For jobs which are team efforts, it may be hard to isolate the contribution of an individual member of the team, to decide whether or not that team member has really met the "goal."

If done well, goal-setting procedures can be useful for the human resource department's goals. They are defensible in court because they're highly job relevant; however, they lack something in comparativeness, because strictly speaking, the same standard is not being applied to all employees with the same job title. For feedback, coaching, counseling, and improving of overall job performance, they're probably the best single performance appraisal technique; but they are inadequate by themselves. In the chapters ahead I will recommend a hybrid system that combines the best features of goal-setting procedures, trait rating, critical-incident methods, and behaviorally based appraisals.

CHAPTER THREE

What Goes Wrong and Why: Eight Common Appraisal Errors

Apart from the strengths and weaknesses inherent in the nature of a given performance appraisal system, there are errors of implementation that can be made no matter what techniques you use. In fact, the way your performance appraisal system is administered, and the training given to the managers using it, probably has more to do with the effectiveness of the appraisal than any other factor. Some performance appraisal systems prevent or reduce these errors more than others, but all are subject to some of them.

The eight most common appraisal errors are:

1. Inadequately defined standards of performance
2. Over-emphasis on recent performance
3. Reliance on gut feelings
4. Miscomprehension of performance standards by employee
5. Insufficient or unclear performance documentation

6. Inadequate time allotment for the discussion
7. Too much talking by manager/supervisor
8. Lack of follow-up plan

INADEQUATELY DEFINED
STANDARDS OF PERFORMANCE

Whatever we call it—the standard or the definition of quality—what is expected must be defined if the performance appraisal is to have any meaning for the employee, for the organization, and for the rating manager.

If at the end of the year as rating manager I say to an individual, "I don't think you're trying hard enough," the employee can reply, "Compared to what? What was the standard against which you held me? How do I know what you expect of me? If I was performing up to the standard, how would you know it, and how could I prove it?" If I can't answer those questions, I don't just have a disgruntled employee, I have a potentially invalid performance appraisal. A clear and measurable idea of effective or superior job performance is the indispensable basis for any performance appraisal. Yet, all too often, it's missing. Managers need to know what they expect of their employees, otherwise evaluations can't be made or defended at the end of the appraisal period.

OVER-EMPHASIS ON RECENT PERFORMANCE

If a manager isn't gathering data over the appraisal period, inevitably, whatever happened in the beginning tends to get pushed back further and further into memory, and he or she winds up basing the appraisal on the events of the most recent month or two.

Some of you are familiar with this as the "Christmas phenomenon": Service providers tend to be more attentive much as children are on their best behavior right around Christmas time, when they know they're in the process of being evaluated. Well, employees know the same thing. A month or two prior to their appraisal they're likely to be on their best behavior. They make lots of suggestions, come in on time, and tend to be responsive to suggestions.

It may seem like an obvious ploy, but it works. It's not just that the manager tends to forget what happened more than a few months ago, it's also, a matter of wishful thinking. Maybe there was a problem with this employee's performance earlier in the year, but now, apparently, it's solved. Why hold it against them, and why bring it up? In fact, employees themselves remember what happened in the past month or two more readily than events that occurred nine months ago, or see the "distant" past as less relevant. Needless to say, this tendency leads to a flawed and inaccurate appraisal.

It's just as inaccurate, by the way, if the employee happens to be having some difficulty at the time the appraisal is completed and you give insufficient emphasis to the early part of the year. Either way you're being overly influenced by a particular moment in time, which may be very misleading. It's certainly not the balanced picture that you want to record.

The only way to counteract this psychological tendency is for the manager to conscientiously record data throughout the year, and to base his or her conclusions on what is in the record, rather than on how the employee has performed lately. The challenge is to know what is being looked for, and have a disciplined approach to collecting information throughout the year.

RELIANCE ON GUT FEELINGS

Gut reactions to an employee's performance or behavior is not irrelevant. There's nothing wrong with taking into account a general sense of employees, how able they are and how hard they're trying. However, these reactions are, by themselves, notoriously untrustworthy, not legally defensible, and not much use when it comes to giving feedback to the employee. The manager needs to be able to say: "I don't think you're trying hard enough. This is what I mean by trying hard enough. Here's my evidence that in fact you have not met the standard that we agreed upon at the beginning of the year." There must be some evidence to back up a gut reaction, otherwise employees will argue, especially if they don't even know what is being said. In fact there's no likely benefit that's going to come from giving gut reactions even if they are correct.

And sometimes, with evidence, you find your gut reaction is modified by the facts.

MISCOMPREHENSION OF PERFORMANCE STANDARDS BY EMPLOYEE

Now let's suppose clear standards of performance *have* been established. The manager knows what is expected of the employees, but the employees have not explained it to *them*. How likely are they to measure up?

If employees aren't given an adequate explanation of the standards by which they're being evaluated, the ratings at the end of the year, even if accurate, may be seen as unfair. Employees may even feel tricked, but most of all, they may not perform well in the first place, because they didn't have a target or benchmark to guide them.

The ideal performance management process set forth in the chapters that follow takes into account the entire appraisal period. As we'll see, the annual performance appraisal meeting is only one step. A good manager coaches, counsels, monitors, and develops his or her employees all through the year. It's possible to do that only by making goals and standards very clear to the employees and keeping these goals in the forefront of their minds.

As mentioned earlier, in many organizations the performance appraisal is the only way employees learn what is expected of them. Even if that's not true in your organization, the performance appraisal is your chance to fine-tune that communication.

Employees should know not only what the standard is, but also, at least in a general way, how judgments are reached. Such an understanding on their part will go a long way toward winning the employees' cooperation in the appraisal process and reducing their defensiveness in the performance appraisal discussion.

INSUFFICIENT OR UNCLEAR PERFORMANCE DOCUMENTATION

It should be obvious that adequate, ongoing documentation is a necessity if a rating manager wants to have more than gut reactions or memory to guide the appraisal. Yet of all the performance appraisal errors failing to document performance is the most common for two reasons: (1) Managers often experience a shortage of time and energy for a chore that may not seem as important when the performance appraisal is a year away as it will seem when it's just around the corner. In this respect the performance appraisal is like anything else: paying attention to details and doing your homework pays off.

(2) Managers seem to share a widespread ambivalence about the appraisal process as a whole. Often managers are reluctant to write down anything negative about an employee. Even if they're not hesitant to confront the employee with the problem, they may still think: "Why write it down? Why let it go into the permanent record where it will follow them around for as long as they work here?" To ask these questions is to ask whether performance appraisals should be done at all. Of course I believe they should be done, and that they should be done as accurately and thoroughly as possible; but the goal is communication, not paperwork.

I would even argue that documenting performance problems represents a higher form of mercy than keeping them out of the record. A performance record in which accurate positive and negative factors are mentioned, will give a balanced picture that may actually be a better picture than the one in which negative factors have been tactfully neglected. It's certainly a necessary basis for a plan that will go to work on this employee's developmental needs.

Before a manager gives an individual employee "a break," he or she should consider how it will affect everyone else in the organization. It's clearly not fair to other employees to fail to distinguish between adequate and inadequate performance. Needless to say, if an employee is at last fired for incompetence and the case has to be defended in court, an accurate record will be important. For that matter, suppose the manager at last finds it necessary to take disciplinary action on that individual. If the documentation states that for the past three or four years the employee has been "fully successful," how will he or she justify that action? "Well, I thought I could motivate the employee by giving him a better appraisal than he deserved, but it didn't work." The greater the legal constraints and scrutiny under which a manager operates, the more the documentation has to reflect the actual events.

If, on the other hand, an employee is advanced or promoted on the basis of too gentle a performance appraisal, a future manager may one day call the employee's present manager and ask: "What did you *do* to me?"

A poorly documented appraisal can also hinder an employee's advancement. If there is an opportunity elsewhere in the organization, that department manager will look through each candidate's file. If an employee's strengths and assets are not presented clearly and accurately he or she may not get considered. Now everyone loses. Managers must be sure positive performance is also documented as well.

INADEQUATE TIME ALLOTMENT FOR THE DISCUSSION

It doesn't take long to do a performance appraisal, if you're just going to take the form and read it to the employee verbatim. Or hand it to them and say, "Please read this and respond." I pointed out how painful the process could be—this is undoubtedly the least painful approach; but it's also the least useful.

I know of one organization whose regular practice was to have its managers write the appraisal and send it to the employee through interoffice mail with the note, "Please sign and return as soon as possible." Well, that doesn't take much time! However a manager isn't going to get a lot of behavior change out of that. Oh, if the manager's only intention was to give a report card or a grade, then perhaps it would not be unreasonable to do it this way. If, however, the manager wants to use the performance appraisal as a vehicle to develop employees, help them improve in their current job, and perhaps increase their opportunity for advancement or promotion, then he or she must schedule enough time to discuss the employee's performance in depth. By this I don't mean merely giving the employee the evaluation, but having a *dialogue* about the implications of the appraisal. Which brings us to our next point. . . .

TOO MUCH TALKING BY MANAGER/SUPERVISOR

This criticism might seem paradoxical to you. After all, isn't the point of the performance appraisal discussion to let the employee know how he or she has done? The employee is being told, right? However, to get the most out of the discussion, a manager needs to listen as well as talk. The manager may have completed the appraisal, but there are still things he or she may need to know. This discussion is a chance to get at the root of performance problems. To make the appraisal motivating for the employee the manager needs to know what that employee is thinking and feeling and to listen *carefully* to what the employee is saying. Good interviewing as well as presentation skills are needed here.

In the selection process, as you may know, if the interviewer does most of the talking, he or she is not learning very much; the same thing is true in the performance appraisal process. If, as manager, I am doing too much talking I am mainly giving my summary. If I can get the employee to respond, I may find out that he or she grudgingly agrees or accepts what I say even if he or she is not happy to hear it. I can get the individual to explain *why* things haven't happened: together we can evolve problem solvers and some kind of plan on which we can both agree.

So managers need to get the employee involved, and to do that they have to get the employee to talk more. Later I'll introduce the mechanisms—listening skills and probing techniques—to draw employees out of their shells.

LACK OF FOLLOW-UP PLAN

If as manager I've done everything right, but there's no follow up plan, it's less likely that I'm going to meet my objectives. So I need to formalize a plan for improving their performance in the employee's current job, if that's necessary, and then, potentially, improving their capacity to advance and grow. I also need to talk with employees about how they can keep, support, and advance the mission of the organization over the coming performance period. Having some kind of follow up plan makes it more likely that that's going to happen.

PART II

Recommended Approach to Performance Management

CHAPTER FOUR

The Swan Approach to Performance Management

The present chapter introduces the performance appraisal program I recommend to my clients; to be more precise, it's an ideal version of that program, which I usually adapt to the particular circumstances of each organization. It's based on the observation that every job has two components: behaviors and activities or objectives. No performance appraisal program can give a balanced picture of performance unless it addresses itself to both these aspects of the job.

1. Behaviors: How do employees do their job on an ongoing basis? What's the standard by which we measure their performance of these ongoing duties? Some sophisticated performance appraisal systems refer to these standards as "competencies."

   These behaviors, or at least the standards by which we measure them, are usually the same for

every employee in a given role. Many of them
are the same for every employee in the organization. The "Performance Factors," discussed in
more detail in Chapter Six, address this ongoing
behavioral aspect of the job.
2. Performance Activities or Objectives: Some objectives are unique and different from one appraisal period to the next. It's quite possible that
you may manage several employees in the same
role, all of whom would be responsible for completely different goals or objectives during a given
appraisal period. The performance objectives,
discussed in greater detail in Chapter Five, address this changing flexible aspect of job performance. These performance objectives have the
additional advantage of helping you to use the
performance appraisal as an active part of the
managerial process: at the beginning of each appraisal period, you can coordinate employee responsibilities with your plans for the coming year,
by building their unique contributions into your
strategy for this year's department or unit performance objectives.

   There's another unique feature to this performance appraisal program. As shown in the diagram
that follows and the form given at the end of this
chapter, this program is basically a two part process.
First, there's the report card phase (this covers Part
I, Part II, and Part III of the form). During this
phase, rating managers give employees feedback on
their performance with reference to the performance
objectives (focused activities) and the performance
factors (the ongoing job requirements) set at the
beginning of the year. This phase measures the past,
and is where most performance appraisals stop. The
method set forth in this chapter goes beyond this

point, however, to a second phase, which concerns the future (Parts IV and V of the form).

First, in Part IV of the form, the development plan concerns a plan for improving employee performance by setting an agreed-on series of tasks for which the employee will not be directly rated. The goal of the development plan may be to bring employees up to standard, to prepare them for advancement, or job enrichment. In Part V of the form, the manager works out with the employee next year's performance plan by establishing and agreeing on the performance objectives for next year.

Phase 1 (The Report Card)

I. OBJECTIVES

How successful the employee was at meeting special goals agreed to at the beginning of the Appraisal Period (as modified or adjusted during that period).

II. PERFORMANCE FACTORS

How the employee did their job during the appraisal period as measured against standards or competencies reflecting identified organization wide core values and the needs of this role.

III. OVERALL EVALUATION FOR THIS APPRAISAL PERIOD

A summary evaluation based on Part I and Part II.

Phase 2 (Planning for the Future)

IV. THE DEVELOPMENT PLAN

A. Ways to improve employees' effectiveness in their current job—this section should include a specific

plan for how employees can improve in areas identified as needing strengthening in the "report card
phase."
B. A plan to provide preparatory experiences for advancement or promotion, so the employee is ready
if and when opportunities open up. Alternatively
(if advancement is not likely or of interest to the
employee) a plan to enrich the employee's experience of the every day job.

V. PERFORMANCE PLAN

New performance objectives are set for the next appraisal period. These performance objectives move the
organization or department forward and are linked with
organization/department goals and objectives. These
objectives become the objectives listed on Part I of the
form at the next performance appraisal. If they are
modified or adjusted during the year, the final modified
version becomes the objectives listed in Part I.

These, then, are the basic elements of the performance management form I recommend, each of
which I'll be discussing in greater detail over the
next few chapters. But to show you how my performance management program functions as a whole,
even in an overview, it isn't enough merely to give
you a form or list the elements. As chemistry professors like to tell us, all the elements of the human
body, separately, would be worth only a few dollars.
It's how they're put together that counts. The same
is true of performance management. It's a *process*,
not a form or a grab bag of appraisal techniques. To
appreciate the usefulness of this approach you have
to see how these elements are played off each other
throughout the appraisal period and beyond it.

EIGHT STEPS OF PERFORMANCE MANAGEMENT

Performance management is not a single event. It
continues throughout the appraisal period and when

the appraisal period is over, performance management doesn't come to an end; it goes on. Therefore the eight-step process presented here forms a circle. Step Eight of this year's appraisal period happens at the same meeting as step one of the next year's appraisal.

1. Performance plan and development plan are agreed to by manager and employee.
2. On-going feedback, coaching, counseling, and documentation are maintained for the next year.
3. As time of appraisal approaches and prior to writing the performance appraisal, manager solicits employee's self-evaluation.
4. Manager meets with the employee to discuss employee's self-evaluation.
5. Manager completes the "report card" portion (Parts I through III) of the performance appraisal form.
6. Manager previews appraisal with his or her manager or human resources.
7. Manager schedules appraisal meeting with employee.
8. Manager conducts appraisal discussion.

Of steps one through four, some may seem too obvious to be regarded as separate steps, others may strike you as unnecessary or overly time-consuming. However, if you bear with me for now, I believe I can show you that all of them make an invaluable contribution to the process, rendering it both more effective and more efficient.

Step 1: Performance Plan and Development Plan Are Agreed to by Manager and Employee

The manager sets performance objectives and hammers out a performance plan with the employee in the appraisal discussion. A development plan is also agreed to, and the standards of performance for the performance factors are clarified.

Step 2: Year-Long On-Going Feedback, Coaching, Counseling, and Documentation

Throughout the following year, the manager conducts periodic informal or formal feedback sessions. The manager documents incidents relevant to the employee's performance, letting the employee know how he or she is progressing with respect to the goals set and performing with respect to the agreed-on standards. If necessary, the manager intervenes to improve performance or to offer coaching and counseling.

Step 3: As Time of Appraisal Approaches and Prior to Writing the Performance Appraisal, Manager Solicits the Employee's Self-Evaluation

This is intended to prepare the employee for the appraisal discussion as well as to provide the manager with an additional source of input when writing the appraisal. The employee is *not* being asked to write his or her own appraisal. The employee should be given adequate time to complete the self-evaluation and provided with a copy of last year's appraisal, if necessary. A copy of a blank performance appraisal form may help an employee collect thoughts regarding current performance, significant work assignments, or how well objectives are being met.

Step 4: Manager Meets With the Employee to Discuss Employee's Self-Evaluation

Still prior to writing the appraisal, manager and employee meet to review the employee's self-evaluation. The primary goal of this meeting is to get information from the employee. The manager's questions or comments should only help to clarify, not challenge. This is not the time to discuss the merits of that individual's view or the final evaluation at this meeting. The input should be seen as an aid in writing the appraisal and preparing for the appraisal discussion.

Step 5: Manager Completes the "Report Card" Portion (Parts I Through III) of the Performance Appraisal Form

Use all the sources of information available, including:

1. The performance data you've gathered throughout the review period.
2. The employee's input.
3. Feedback from internal and/or external sources (customers, vendors, etc.) where appropriate.

Step 6: Manager Previews Appraisal With His or Her Manager or Human Resources

Organization policies often dictate that appraisals be previewed by the next level of management prior to your meeting with the employee, and generally speaking, it is a good idea. It insures understanding and agreement. The human resources department may also be involved in this step.

Even if it is not required by your administrative procedures, this is a very useful step for a number of reasons. For one thing, your own manager is one step removed from the interaction, and can bring a fresh perspective to it. You know what you meant by what you wrote; it may not be apparent to you that it has another interpretation; having someone else review before you present it to the employee may help catch that interpretation and prevent misunderstanding, embarrassment or an argument. Then, too, a manager one level up may be in a better position than you to make sure that your procedures are in line with organization policy. Finally, your manager or a representative from human resources can check the legal ramifications of the appraisal.

Step 7: Manager Schedules Appraisal Meeting with Employee

The manager sets a date, time, and place for the meeting that will give both parties an opportunity to focus on the appraisal without interruption. There should be enough time for the entire appraisal and development discussion.

Step 8: Manager Conducts the Appraisal Discussion

The manager discusses the completed appraisal and development plan with the employee. The manager should maintain control but give ample opportunity for discussion.

The employee should be given an opportunity to write comments into the record if he or she wishes. The employee's signature affirms only his or her participation in the process; it affirms that the performance appraisal has taken place, not necessarily that he or she agrees with its content.

During this same meeting you'll work out the performance plan for the next year—thus, Step 8 of the process blends into Step 1.

HOW THIS PROGRAM COMPARES WITH THE OTHER PROGRAMS SURVEYED IN CHAPTER TWO

As shown by our review of the most commonly used appraisal techniques in Chapter Two, no single performance appraisal technique is the best at doing everything most organizations want appraisals to do. No single technique is the fairest, most comparative, most accurate, and most defendable. No single technique is the best for salary administration *and* solving performance problems *and* implementing the goals of the manager who must help administer the program. That's why the performance management program I recommend is a hybrid, combining the best methods covered in Chapter Two, methods that complement and strengthen each other (Figure 4.1).

In fact, there are only two techniques covered in Chapter Two that do *not* make a contribution to the program I've just outlined: *peer-ranking procedures* (Method 3), which as we saw were really more a way of presenting information than a way of appraising performance; and the *global essay* technique (Method 1) although, as we'll see in Chapter Nine, I do recommend that your evaluation contain narrative elements.

The performance factors of my recommended technique are closely related to the trait-rating scales (Method 2), although the standards I recommend using are less personal and more behavioral; they also have strong affinities with BARS (Method 6).

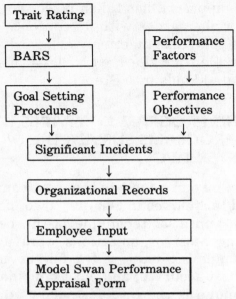

FIGURE 4.1 The contribution of the various basic techniques to the Swan program.

The performance objectives are identical to the "Objectives and Goal-Setting Procedures" (Method 7) described in Chapter Two.

My program also makes use of organizational records (Method 4) and significant incidents (Method 3). However, instead of providing a sole basis for the appraisal, these methods function as sources of data to inform and substantiate the conclusions reached as to how the employee measured against the performance factors and performance objectives. As an additional source of information, as well as to help ensure employee "buy-in" to the process, my program makes use of employee input—an element not including among the techniques covered in Chapter Four.

In the coming chapters I'm going to focus much more closely on the individual parts and steps involved in the program, but first I'd like to take some time to deal with the questions that come up at this point when I'm presenting this approach to a live audience.

THE ADVANTAGES AND DISADVANTAGES OF THE SYSTEM

Is This Approach to Performance Management Too Time-Consuming?

The most frequent initial objection raised by participants in my "How to Conduct the Performance Appraisal" seminars to the process just outlined is that it's too time-consuming. For some manager-employee relationships in some organizations this is the sober truth. If a manager is personally in charge of performance appraisals for hundreds of employees, most of whom he or she speaks to only 15 minutes out of the year, then obviously not much time can be invested with each employee in the performance management process. Of course I would suggest that in this event the manager is probably not the person who should be doing the performance appraisal. It should be borne in mind that the system presented in this chapter is an ideal, and is offered to those who are in a position to implement it. I will deal with other realities in a later chapter.

In any case, the question remains, *is* this approach really time-consuming, considering what it accomplishes and comparing it to other commonly used performance appraisal techniques?

The time-consuming aspect of this approach to performance management derives from a greater number of contacts between manager and employee, more input from employee, more time spent discussing goals and expectations and in monitoring the ways employees measure up. But look what you get out of this "extra time" . . .

No Surprises

How much easier a manager's task would be if he or she never had to announce to a startled employee at the end of the year that that individual's performing below expectations. Eliminating that awkwardness is one of the advantages of a performance management process in which specific goals and standards are set at the beginning of the appraisal period. These goals and standards provide a context and structure for all subsequent interactions with employees. On a daily, weekly, or monthly basis the manager can meet with the employee and say: "At the beginning of the year we said this was our target; let's see how we're doing towards that. Well, it looks like we're diverting a little bit. What further help can I give you, or what can we do. . . . ?"

If a manager works with the employee all year round, using as a constant reference the performance factors and objectives set with the employee at the beginning of the year, the appraisal itself won't be a traumatic event for either party. In fact, both will have a pretty good idea what's going to be on the form ahead of time; the performance appraisal will merely be the formalization of what's happened all year long.

Connecting Employee Performance With the Personal Goals and the Goals of the Organization

There are organizational, division, and departmental goals that managers are expected to meet, and perhaps the most important measure of a manager's effectiveness is his or her ability to connect employees' performance with those goals. After all, the job of a manager is to get things done through other

people. The performance management process outlined here is an ideal vehicle for achieving that objective. As we'll see in the next chapter "Setting
Good Performance Objectives," the targets a manager sets for employees at the beginning of the year
don't merely provide bench marks for measuring employee performance or improvement, they are an
opportunity to coordinate the efforts of the employees, assuring that every one of them is contributing
to a greater overall strategy.

This focus is often the missing piece in the way
managers direct their employees. As manager I may
say to an employee, "Well, what would you like to
do next year," or "Here's an area in which I think
you could do better," or "I heard about this training
program, it may be useful to you." But often what
the employee works on is not connected with what
we're trying to accomplish around here, with what
we're doing as a department or as an organization.
The performance appraisal becomes a much more
powerful tool if it connects things the manager ex-
pects of the employee with the goals required or to
which he aspires.

Clarity

If, like most managers, I receive as well as conduct
performance appraisals, I can ask myself: wouldn't
it be nice to know, at the beginning of each appraisal
period, exactly what's expected of me? With this
program, at the beginning of the year and throughout the year it's crystal clear how I'm going to be
evaluated. I know what I need to accomplish to be
considered exceeding expectations, what level of
performance would be meeting expectations, and what
would fall below expectations.

With clear objectives and standards set forth at

the beginning of the appraisal period all tasks and appraisals will be easier and less anxiety producing for the employees. It would enable them on a daily basis to know where they stand.

This performance management program, with its greater degree of interaction with the employee, also makes clear for employees how to go about meeting these objectives. That's the difference between performance *planning* and just setting objectives and then saying at the end of the year "Well, let's look at how well you did toward those objectives." The plan actually includes the mechanisms by which those objectives are to be met.

Employee Development

The extra time spent with employees at the beginning of the year can make enormous difference to their sense of involvement, their enthusiasm, their understanding of the opportunities available for learning, advancement to new positions, or enrichment of their current job.

True, *career development* is a category that doesn't apply to every employee, but it may have wider application than you think. Some employees may know they are going to leave the organization in a few years. Other employees may not seem to be interested in growing beyond their present position (this is not necessarily negative, by the way). True, employee development wouldn't apply to these individuals if we define development as motivating them to move to the next level or dramatically increasing their productivity; but managers can do things to enrich their everyday experience of the job. They can give employees more interesting things to do, more support and more encouragement. Managers should also encourage employees to give us their input; they probably have some ideas that might be useful. (Ten million Japanese workers, asked their opinion about how things could be done better for one half hour every two weeks for ten years, yielded productivity improvement we marvel at today in Japan). The performance appraisal can help accomplish these goals.

About five years ago the management of a large western bank found that many employees at a middle to senior management level were leaving in large numbers, and they assumed that it was because the company wasn't doing well and people were just jumping ship. I was involved in a survey done at that time. Data collected through internal interviewing showed that a large proportion of the individuals who were leaving were doing so not because the company was having problems, but because they felt that management no longer cared about them. "What makes you think that?" these employees were asked. They replied, "Well, nobody's talking to me." The managers who were no longer talking to their employees said, "What's the point of talking to my employees, I can't give them the opportunity to advance, because such opportunities are restricted now."

Moral: the very act of speaking with employees, even if you can't offer them advancement (or even if they're not interested in advancement) is still valuable because it gives them the sense that they're important. It keeps them working at the highest level in their current job, it shows that they have not been forgotten, and it gives a manager the opportunity to learn things from them that might be helpful. It's so simple and powerful a concept, yet so often ignored or neglected, even in our personal life.

Coaching and Counseling

The goals, targets, and objectives set up in the beginning of the appraisal period provide the context for coaching and counseling of employees during the year. Without them, there's no basis for coaching. In football it's clear what the goal is; in the context of a complex job it's less clear what is expected on a daily basis unless some goals and targets are set up front and broken down into elements. If during the course of the year they're not fulfilling some of the goals and expectations, these same goals set at the beginning give the manager the mechanism to handle the problem. The greater the degree of employee–management interaction built into a performance management program the easier and smoother this intervention will tend to be.

WHY GET EMPLOYEE INPUT RIGHT BEFORE THE APPRAISAL

The past five years or so has seen the emergence of a strong trend toward involving employees in decisions affecting their life at work. In the automotive industry, for example, where people were once hired to perform repetitive tasks and expected to keep their mouths shut, employees are now being encouraged and invited to make suggestions in an effort to improve their commitment to the quality of the product. Ford Motor Company calls their program "employee involvement." This trend is sometimes attributed to the influence of Japanese style management on American business; but that's only part of the story. The Japanese took 1950s industrial and organization psychology and simply applied it, while we ignored it. Now we're learning it from the Japanese.

The same logic is also being applied today, with remarkable success, to performance management programs. A perennial problem of the performance appraisal is that its recipients are usually very disdainful of the process, and the most common reason is that it does not include them. At the end of the year their manager sits down and gives them a report card. Their opinion was not solicited, and they did not have a chance to give their side of the story. Why should they work with the manager toward solving a performance "problem" they may not even agree they have? By contrast, when employees have the opportunity, before the form is completed, to give information to the manager that will be taken into account along with other information, they find the process much more credible.

A manager may not be comfortable with the idea of involving the employee in the appraisal up front. It does require more time and an additional meeting with the employee. Yet it has tremendous advantages. First of all, it isn't just something you do merely as a concession to the employees, to make them feel good. It's an additional source of data, adding to the appraisal's accuracy. It makes sure that all the relevant facts are taken into account. For all the manager knows, he or she may have forgotten something that should have been considered and the employee can remind you. It could be awkward if an important mitigating factor comes up in the final performance appraisal discussion, after the appraisal is signed by one or two upper managers. All the facts should be in before anyone signs the appraisal. If there is going to be some disagreement between manager and employee during the later performance meeting, it would be better to find out in advance. This gives the manager time to marshall his or her evidence. He or she can characterize the facts more carefully, knowing the employee has a different view. "Now, based upon our discussion earlier, I know that you feel somewhat differently about this. Let me, however, show you how I came to my conclusion." Without the earlier meeting, the manager may get to the final performance appraisal discussion, mention an issue, only to discover they have a totally different perception. Because it's the first time he or she has heard of the employee's view, the manager has to scramble and think fast. Thus, not only will the employee be more on the defensive, perhaps the manager will too. When the manager gets employee's input in advance, in many cases the net result will be more efficient and less time consuming, because the actual performance appraisal discussion is much briefer and more to the point after this preliminary meeting.

Of course this process needs to be modified in special cases. In systems and data processing positions, scientific project work, and even in the audit function, there are specific assignments or projects or engagements throughout the year. Obviously it won't be necessary to solicit the employee's feedback right before the annual appraisal if you've gotten it 15 times during the year. Yet be sure to get their input after *each* project or engagement, so some input is available when the performance appraisal is written.

In most instances, getting the employees feedback prior to writing the performance appraisal is very valuable; managers who have tried it and employees who have experienced it have been pleased with the results.

I don't mean to imply that we're going to avoid disagreements or even direct conflict entirely. There's always the chance that when a manager finally sits down with an employee, no matter how right and how prepared he or she is, the employees will dig in their heels. They know as well as you do that dollars are ultimately connected with the outcome, and they may stand their ground even against the best evidence. The manager still will need to have the skills to deal with defensiveness and conflict, but you can avoid unnecessary misunderstandings. When you meet with employees up front you learn what their hot buttons are. Getting employees' view of their performance before the appraisal generally diminishes conflict, and it certainly helps the manager to manage those conflicts which are inevitable.

One important note of caution is necessary with regard to getting employee input prior to writing the appraisal. It is an abuse of the process to make employees write their own appraisal. The thought that the manager is going to take the employee's self evaluation and rework it as the appraisal is one of the reasons some employees are reluctant to participate—they may have been burned before. Therefore, the manager should make it clear initially that this is not the intention, that the employee's input is one of the sources of information used by the manager to write their appraisal. In fact, the manager should let them know that he or she wants them to use it as a way to prepare for a detailed discussion of their view of their own performance over the next year.

Model Annual Performance Appraisal Form

PART I   Review of Progress Toward Meeting Last Year's Objectives

Objectives Agreed To Last Year (As modified during the year)	Results (Narrative)	Weighting (Must Total 100%)	Rating
1.		____ %	☐ Greatly exceeded standard ☐ Exceeded the standard ☐ Met the standard ☐ Did not meet the standard ☐ Significantly below the standard
2.		____ %	☐ Greatly exceeded standard ☐ Exceeded the standard ☐ Met the standard ☐ Did not meet the standard ☐ Significantly below the standard
3.		____ %	☐ Greatly exceeded standard ☐ Exceeded the standard ☐ Met the standard ☐ Did not meet the standard ☐ Significantly below the standard
4.		____ %	☐ Greatly exceeded standard ☐ Exceeded the standard ☐ Met the standard ☐ Did not meet the standard ☐ Significantly below the standard

5.

☐ ☐ ☐ ☐ ☐

Greatly exceeded standard
Exceeded the standard
Met the standard
Did not meet the standard
Significantly below the standard

——— %

Overall Weighted Average Rating for Objectives ———

PART II Review of Progress Toward Meeting the Standards of Performance Agreed to Last Year

Performance Factors	Weighting (Must Total 100%)	Rating

1.

——— %

☐ ☐ ☐ ☐ ☐

Greatly exceeded standard
Exceeded the standard
Met the standard
Did not meet the standard
Significantly below the standard

2.

——— %

☐ ☐ ☐ ☐ ☐

Greatly exceeded standard
Exceeded the standard
Met the standard
Did not meet the standard
Significantly below the standard

3.

——— %

☐ ☐ ☐ ☐ ☐

Greatly exceeded standard
Exceeded the standard
Met the standard
Did not meet the standard
Significantly below the standard

Model Annual Performance Appraisal Form—(*Continued*)

PART II Review of Progress Toward Meeting the Standards of Performance Agreed to Last Year

Performance Factors	Weighting (Must Total 100%)	Rating
4.	____ %	☐ Greatly exceeded standard ☐ Exceeded the standard ☐ Met the standard ☐ Did not meet the standard ☐ Significantly below the standard
5.	____ %	☐ Greatly exceeded standard ☐ Exceeded the standard ☐ Met the standard ☐ Did not meet the standard ☐ Significantly below the standard
6.	____ %	☐ Greatly exceeded standard ☐ Exceeded the standard ☐ Met the standard ☐ Did not meet the standard ☐ Significantly below the standard
7.	____ %	☐ Greatly exceeded standard ☐ Exceeded the standard ☐ Met the standard ☐ Did not meet the standard ☐ Significantly below the standard

Overall Weighted Average Rating for Performance Factors _____

PART III SUMMARY OF OVERALL PERFORMANCE FOR YEAR

WEIGHTED AVERAGE OF OBJECTIVES AND PERFORMANCE FACTORS

☐ Greatly Exceeded Standard
☐ Exceeded the Standard
☐ Met the Standard
☐ Did not meet the Standard
☐ Significantly below Standard

PART IV DEVELOPMENT PLAN

A. (For use if any individual rating is below "Met the Standard," or if employee wants to work on any area of current job)

For improvement in current job the following actions/objectives have been agreed to:

1.

2.

3.

4.

B. (For use if advancement or career growth is a practical option and employee is interested)

For preparation for possible advancement the following actions/ objectives have been agreed to:

1.

2.

3.

4.

C. (Job enrichment: For use if advancement or career growth is not an option, or if employees is not interested)

The following actions/objectives have been agreed to:

1.

2.

3.

4.

PART V   PERFORMANCE PLAN

The objectives agreed upon by employee and manager for the next year (additions or modifications are to be done in writing). **THESE OBJECTIVES BECOME THE SUBJECT MATTER OF PART I OF THE FORM NEXT YEAR.**

1.

2.

3.

4.

5.

PART VI   EMPLOYEE STATEMENT (Optional — Additional sheets may be used)

PART VII   SIGNATURES

MANAGER (Direct Supervisor)Date

INITIALS
PRIOR TO
APPRAISAL
DISCUSSION
(_____)

DEPARTMENT MANAGER   Date

EMPLOYEE   Date
(Signature acknowledges that this form
has been reviewed with employee. It does
not imply agreement with content.)

INITIALS
PRIOR TO
APPRAISAL
DISCUSSION
(_____)

HUMAN RESOURCES   Date

CHAPTER FIVE

Setting Good Performance Objectives

In this chapter and the one after it, I'll be showing you how to *create* and effectively *use* performance objectives and performance factors, the two aspects of total job performance which form the core of the performance appraisal method recommended in this book.

The word "create" applies mainly to the performance objectives covered in this chapter. Performance objectives and development objectives are set and reset each year by the manager working in cooperation with the employee (or at least with the input and acknowledgment of the employee). Identifying or naming performance factors, by contrast is seldom up to the discretion of the individual manager, although managers may have wide latitude in defining the performance factors, setting the standard of performance, and deciding on their relative weight. Performance factors are organization-wide values evolving out of top management decisions made when a performance management program is first instituted.

A performance management program that makes use of performance objectives gives extra responsibility to the manager. In order to make the program work, the manager must be able to set meaningful performance objectives, possibly different ones for each appraisal period.

It's an effort that pays off. Establishing good performance objectives is not only the key to a fair and accurate performance appraisal, it's an effective way to direct employees, to coordinate their efforts so they contribute to the achievement of departmental goals and those of the entire organization.

CHARACTERISTICS OF A GOOD PERFORMANCE OBJECTIVE

First of all, performance objectives are specific potential achievements of the employee. They may be either basic or grand. As opposed to performance factors, objectives are to be met within a specific, previously agreed upon time-frame. Often, by the end of the appraisal period, a performance objective will be *over*. Performance factors, on the other hand, are permanent features of the ongoing job. They concern standards of performance that apply to every action the employee takes on the job.

It's entirely possible that, with any given job, the performance factors and performance objectives might both concern the same tasks. In this case, the performance objectives will be framed in such a way as to concern *what* the employee does; the performance factors will be more concerned with *how* those tasks are accomplished.

For example, a job description might define an audit manager's responsibility this way: "Conducts audits at the direction of Comptroller in a timely, accurate, and professional manner." The description is certainly clear, but phrased this way, it's neither a factor nor an objective. It's just a job requirement.

Suppose we take that same job requirement, focus on the individual audit manager, and apply it to the organization's goal of achieving greater efficiency. We could then write the following performance objective: "In the next year, reduce the time budget for five audits by 10%." The job requirement has been used to create a specific measurable objective. It happens over a specific period of time. It will be easy to decide whether—and when—the performance objective was met.

Performance objectives that are vague or hard to measure can lead to misunderstandings and poor performance. To be useful, performance objectives must be clear, measurable, and easily understood. Take the following example:

Design new products using microwave technology.

This is not a clear performance objective. It's vague, it's easily misunderstood, and can't be measured. Design what new products? How many? By when? Compare that with—

Complete design within 12 months for an XYZ tube with a minimum operating life of 24,000 hours and a maximum production cost of $10,000 per tube.

A manager would undoubtedly give the employees more direction than is found in the above sentence; but at least it contains the basic criteria for deciding, at the end of the appraisal period, whether the task has been accomplished or not. It's clearly stated. It can be measured. It's based on actions and results that are easily observed.

A good way of gauging the usefulness of any performance objective would be to see whether it meets the criteria in the following checklist. A performance objective should be

1. Focused on specific results to be achieved rather than the general tasks, duties, or expectations of the ongoing job
2. Significant
3. Realistic, but requires "stretch"
4. Specific and measurable
5. Prioritized and weighted
6. Clearly worded and measurable
7. Limited to a few in number
8. Synchronized with the organization, division, or department objectives

Focused on Specific Results To Be Achieved Rather Than the General Tasks, Duties, or Expectations of the Ongoing Job

This is the chief distinction between a performance objective and a performance factor. Consider the following examples:

> *Respond to customer requests for service by telephone contact or on-site call on a next business day basis.*

> *Create a plan by June 1, 199X to predict monthly inventory levels of raw material levels necessary to meet production demands based on orders received by the first of that month. Plan must predict minimum inventory necessary, with no more than 5% remainder after each production cycle.*

Enter monthly sales orders into the computer system by the 5th working day of each month.

The first and the third of these examples are *performance factors*. They describe tasks which are undoubtedly permanent features of the job. Only the second example, "Create a plan by June 1, 199X . . ." is a task with an *end in sight*.

It's entirely possible, of course, that the employee might have to achieve that goal (create a new plan or modify the old one) more than once. In that case, it might be a performance objective in more than one performance appraisal period. However, it's still a performance objective as long as it doesn't need to be done every month or every quarter or as long as the performance objective can be phrased in such a way that the employee knows the exact number of times the task must be done (i.e., "Determine the minimum inventory level 5 times within the next year" as opposed to "Determine the minimum inventory level whenever it's required"). If it's not an ongoing general task or responsibility, it's a performance objective.

Significant

Performance objectives must have *importance*. If they aren't important, why set them? Performance objectives are not arbitrary hurdles set up for employees to provide a basis for rating them. They're a way of integrating the employee's performance with personal goals and the larger strategies of the organization. That can't happen in any meaningful way unless the performance objectives are important enough to make a difference to the overall effort.

Realistic, but Requires "Stretch"

Undoubtedly, the tougher an assignment, the harder
it will be to get employees to agree to it, and the
greater the chance they'll resist it. That's why some
managers set performance objectives (or their
equivalent within other performance management
programs) that employees can do in their sleep. This
practice is particularly common in small stable organizations where everybody knows each other and
has worked together for many years. It's understandable, but it's a mistake.

Setting performance objectives that are too easy
won't do much for increasing your department's productivity, and it certainly won't get your own goals
met (unless you do everything yourself).

Specific and Measurable

Specificity and measurability are characteristics that
should be found, to the maximum degree possible,
in everything that goes on a performance appraisal
form. The more specific and measurable performance objectives are, the clearer they can be made
to employees. In addition there's likely to be less
dispute over whether and how well the objectives
were met. Such performance objectives are also more
defendable in any legal action.

In some jobs, inevitably, there will be factors that
are important to the employee's effectiveness that
seem hard to measure and hard to make specific. I
certainly do not recommend ignoring them just because they're hard to measure. If they're important
job requirements, they should have a place on the
performance appraisal. The trick is to find out how
to make these job requirements as specific and measurable as possible (see Chapter Six.). Happily, per-

formance objectives, by their very nature, are limited in scope, so they can more easily be made specific. Because managers have more freedom to choose and create performance objectives for each performance period, there's no reason why every performance objective shouldn't be specific and measurable.

Prioritized and Weighted

Common sense suggests that when you send an employee off to meet seven complex performance objectives it would be a good idea to at least list them in order of importance ("weight"). It would also be a good idea to mention which should be done first, if they're not going to all be done simultaneously ("prioritize"). Each employee should know at the beginning of the year not only what is expected, but the priorities and weightings of these performance objectives so he or she can make decisions independently on a daily basis at every fork in the road.

Weighting is also of considerable importance when it comes to arriving at an overall evaluation of the employee's performance at the end of the appraisal period. To give an accurate depiction of the requirements of most jobs, it's not enough to list the tasks of the job. All of the tasks and behaviors may be important, but some of them are more important than others, and for that matter, some of them come into play 90% of the time while others come into play only 10% of the time. The manager needs some way to express that difference on the appraisal. Weighting the items gives the manager that ability. Therefore, at the beginning of the appraisal period, when the manager is deciding on performance objectives and discussing them with your employee, he or she should also decide on and discuss the weighting of each performance objective.

Clearly Worded and Measurable

Effective, well written performance objectives contain these four elements: TO (action verb) / RESULTS / BY WHEN (date) / STANDARD (cost or other quantifier)
For example:

"To reduce overtime in the XYZ unit from 150 hours/month to 50 hours/month by December 1, 199X at a cost not to exceed $12,000."

ACTION VERB: "to reduce"

RESULTS: "Overtime from 150 hours/month to 50 hours/month"

BY WHEN: "By December 1, 199X"

STANDARD: "At a cost not to exceed $12,000."

Limited to a Few in Number

Give me twenty critical performance objectives and I probably won't get to them all. Please give me a reasonable number.

For a given employee in a given appraisal period, there could hardly be twenty performance objectives that were all "focused results," "significant," and required that the employee "stretch." If that many occur, the manager should re-think the nature of a performance objective.

What, then, is a reasonable number of non-routine, significant, realistic (but "stretch"-requiring), specific, prioritized, and weighted objectives? I hear the numbers five to ten most often from my clients, and seven would be the average. Of course if there are many areas in which an employee needs improvement in his or her current job, there may be less time and room for the employee to meet any new performance objectives. It might be better to postpone some objectives to another appraisal period. Jobs such as project work that do not lend themselves to large broad accomplishments (such as project work in the systems and data processing department) may require many smaller performance objectives and they may be assigned quarterly or in an as needed basis. Even so the basic criteria of a good performance objective remain the same.

Synchronized with Organization, Division, or Department Objectives

If I make sure that my performance objectives meet this particular criterion, I'll be taking the fullest advantage of the productive power of an objective-based performance management program.

What are we trying to get done around here? What are the things we'd like to improve upon or build towards? What are some of the things that are expected of me as a manager? Out of that and the employee's job description, the employee and I can create our targets.

WHERE DO I GET PERFORMANCE OBJECTIVES?

It may be instantly clear to me, as manager, just what performance objectives would be perfect for a given employee. It may simply be a matter of taking goals and targets that are already set for my employees, re-thinking them in terms of the criteria I've just set forth, and working them into a performance plan. However, if I'm managing employees whose work is routine and unchanging, or unusually autonomous, this may be a new way of thinking about management.

To set measurable, challenging, and achievable performance objectives a manager might utilize the following resources:

1. Previous objectives—from last review period
2. Employee input
3. Job descriptions—specific job duties/task
4. Performance factors
5. Division/department plans, objectives, or strategies.
6. Objectives of next higher level of management
7. Discussions with peer managers, customers, or "internal clients"
8. Organizational problems and opportunities

Previous Performance Plan

Assuming this isn't the first year of the performance appraisal program, the first place to look for this coming year's performance objectives is at last year's performance objectives. They may be just as relevant now; there's no reason why the same performance objective can't be used again. Perhaps some of last year's performance objectives represent the first step toward an accomplishment that will take more than one year. Some of this year's performance objectives can be the second step toward that accomplishment.

Employee Input

When a manager has an employee prepare for that preliminary meeting prior to your writing the appraisal (Step 2 of the eight steps of the performance management program), it's a good idea to ask the employee to think about possible performance objectives for next year. This puts another mind at work on the problem—a mind which is, needless to say, very close to the issues involved. The manager is under no obligation to accept these suggestions, but may find them useful, and the chances are that the employee will work harder to achieve the suggested performance objectives. Of course, either at the end of the formal performance appraisal meeting or in a meeting soon after it, it's a good idea for the manager to get employee input on the assigned performance objectives, whether or not they've arisen out of suggestions the employee has made.

Some managers or supervisors are reluctant to discuss objectives with the employee because they don't want to give the appearance of surrendering their authority. In addition it seems dangerous to give employees a choice. What if they argue? What if they resist? What if they just plain won't do it? However, these problems turn out to be more worrisome in theory than in reality. A manager doesn't give up ultimate authority by talking to the employee about problems and solutions; on the contrary, the manager is making better use of that authority. As for employee resistance: not talking to employees doesn't prevent resistance; it just prevents finding out about it and dealing with it. When a manager simply assigns objectives without discussion that's when the lowest level of compliance from an employee occurs.

Furthermore, when employees discuss objectives with their manager, often they ask questions which help communicate the expectations. An objective which seems crystal clear to the manager may, at first, be completely incomprehensible to the employee; the manager wouldn't find that out except through discussion. By responding to the employee's specific questions, a manager can refine the objectives to the point where they're clear to anyone who reads them.

Job Descriptions

Performance objectives can often be derived by crossing job description requirements with the strategies of the organization. Take a job description requirement such as "making presentations and sales calls to increase the number of leads generated." At first blush we would regard this as a performance factor. It's a routine task, a permanent feature of the job, but under some circumstances a variation of it would be a performance objective. Suppose the organization needs to promote a particular product. One performance objective, arrived at by integrating the job description requirement with the business strategy of the organization, might be: "Do five presentations over the next two months specifically on product." That would be the performance objective; the employee would still be responsible for the performance factor of maintaining an ongoing series of presentations.

For employees that have relatively routine jobs, instead of pulling out performance objectives, the manager might pull out individual tasks from the employee's job description and make them specific and measurable. At least in the subsequent period the employee would be aware of areas of emphasis and focused their energy.

Performance Factors

The performance factors are usually the same for all employees and can be taken to represent the values and aims of the organization. If factors are perceived as values the organization wants to actualize, they can be another possible source of inspiration for specific performance objectives.

Note, however, that I'm not suggesting that the

manager take note of an area of weakness in an employee in relation to a performance factor and set a performance objective of *improving*. That might be a good source of a developmental objective, but not of a performance objective. A performance objective moves the organization forward, not the employee. Instead, the manager should just examine the performance factors. What are they? What do they say about the aims of the organization? For example, a typical performance factor is "quality of work"; because it's been determined that "quality of work" is a critical factor of all employee performance, I might ask myself, "What kind of performance objective can I set with my employee that would improve the quality of work around here (not, however, specifically improving the quality of this individual employee's work. Again, that would be a developmental objective. It moves the employee forward—makes them more effective—but does not directly focus on moving the organization forward in a specific way).

Division/Department Plans, Objectives, or Strategies

Organization, division, and department plans and goals are also key sources for developing employee performance objectives. In fact, performance objectives are simply a logical extension of the annual business planning process. They identify the specific actions and behaviors of employees that will accomplish the department's goals.

Each employee's activity or contribution should support the larger goal desired. The manager/supervisor should be able to demonstrate the relationship between department goals and objectives and the performance objectives of individual employees.

As manager, I would look at what the division or department is trying to get done, and ask myself is there any role this employee can play. Suppose one of the goals of the department this year is "increase customer response time"—that is, to get back to customers more quickly with an answer or solution. Then I say, "Well if that's what we're trying to do, what role can Phil play?" Write a performance objective which associates Phil's activities with advancing that goal.

Objectives of Next Higher Level of Management

There may not be formal department goals or objectives, but by talking to progressively higher levels of management, one can get an idea of what those higher up would like to get done. Imagine what my superiors might think if I went to them and said, "I'd like to know what you want done around here, so I can incorporate those goals into my performance objectives for my employees!"

Discussions with Peer Managers, Customers, or "Internal Clients"

Other managers or supervisors may have employees whose tasks are similar to mine, so they may supply me with some ideas. Doing this has the added value of helping to coordinate tasks laterally.

"Internal clients" may also be useful sources of objectives (systems and data processing departments call them "user groups"; the audit function refers to other departments as "clients"). I might also find it useful to talk to my customers if I have any, regarding what they want, need, or value. This information may suggest focused activities I can assign to one of my employees.

Whatever label I use, the trick is not to write performance objectives in a vacuum. Looking all around at every group with which I interface is the way to write performance objectives that move forward the strategic goals of the organization, division, or department, helps meet the managerial objectives for which the manager is being held accountable, and gives employees a sense of working in some meaningful way on important activities.

Organizational Problems and Opportunities

Most organizations have some ongoing chronic problems. Perhaps there is something that no one is talking about at the department level, but of which everybody is aware. Even if a manager hasn't had direction on it from the top brass, a problem like that can be the source of a performance objective.

Opportunities are events which call for a timely response. Perhaps there's an area in the organization that has just finished a big project. While it was going on people from that area were not receptive to considering changes. The manager might write a performance objective for someone to interface with that area now. A few months ago they were busy and wouldn't have been open to the idea; but now they are—grab this opportunity while it's ripe.

All of these are useful and important sources of performance objectives. You may not need all of them, and you may not have time to use all of them. If you are under extreme time pressure you should at least consult the previous Performance Plan, Job Descriptions, and Employee Input first—these are the sources closest to the nuts and bolts of the job. If a number of employees report to you, you might be able to use all the sources to create a pool of performance objectives and then parcel them out to individual employees.

Performance objectives are first of all assignments that move a manager's plans forward—only secondarily are they tests of employee performance. A manager should first decide what are the tasks to be completed; then look around for people to do them. A completely different set of performance objectives may be given to every employee, or the same performance objective to every employee. There may always be a few performance objectives that will apply to many or all.

CHAPTER SIX

Defining Performance Factors

Performance factors might be broadly defined as the *ways* employees handle all on-going job duties. Both taken together represent the totality of good on-going job performance. For example, it might seem obvious that as a manager I'd be very well pleased if at my direction my employees were to successfully introduce a new product on time and within the pre-set cost constraints. Suppose, however, that in meeting these objectives they alienated key members of another department, making it less likely that I'll have that department's cooperation in the future. Then I wouldn't be as pleased. An organization can't help but be concerned with *how* the job gets done, and this aspect of job performance is best measured by performance factors.

PERFORMANCE FACTORS

The following list outlines the values of performance factors.

1. *Provide managers and employees with consistent definition of quality performance.* What kind of on-the-job behavior goes into doing the job *right*? What are the ingredients? The performance factors not only set a standard to be used to evaluate the employees, they also show employees what to shoot for.
2. *Reinforce the core values of the organization.* Performance factors are generally chosen at the policy-setting level of the organization. They're meant to embody the values the organization considers important. The performance factors can be an organization's way of saying: "These are the values which we want our employees to actualize and through which we want them to represent us; this is what we stand for." It puts the mission statement into action.
3. *Provides coaching tools for improving future performance. How* employees are performing their jobs is precisely what a manager needs to monitor if he or she is going to coach and counsel the employees effectively. If employees are not meeting their performance objectives, there's a good chance that a glance at the way they stack up on the performance *factors* will show what they're doing wrong and why they're not meeting their performance objectives.
4. *Support individual effectiveness and overall organizational performance.* Performance factors are chosen because they work. We know from experience or from analysis of the job that they're important standards of behavior. While performance objectives measure that part of an employee's contribution to the group effort that can be isolated—this individual was clearly responsible for that focused activity or result—asking employees to measure up to standards of perfor-

mance through the performance factors encourages behaviors which are known to be beneficial
in the long run, even when management can't
document their link to an immediate positive outcome.

SOURCES OF PERFORMANCE FACTORS

In some shape or other, by some name or other,
most performance appraisal forms have a component
similar to this "laundry list" of qualities that I am
referring to as performance factors. It's the most
widely used performance appraisal approach.

Ideally, performance factors have been carefully
selected by an organization to reflect those issues or
values which are seen as important. They're job relevant and relevant to the goals of the organization.
Some organizations even include performance factors like "contribution to profitability" or "commitment to affirmative action plan." As a rule they're
set on an organization-wide basis, usually for all employees in a category, (the categories are typically
"exempt" and "non exempt," but sometimes include
Professional/Technical and Manager/Supervisor).
Occasionally there are separate or additional performance factors for technical professionals and
managers.

While as a rule a manager will establish individual
performance objectives in cooperation with each employee at the beginning of the appraisal period, it's
not likely that the individual manager will have the
responsibility of choosing the performance factors
(although he or she will set the standard of performance and weighting for each of them). But in case
you have any input into the decisions that go into
drawing up or altering your organization's list of
performance factors, here are some tips on where

to find performance factors that are specific, job-relevant, and measurable.

Because performance factors are generally desirable permanent characteristics of an employee, managers can arrive at them by analyzing the job requirements the same way they'd analyze it in preparation for hiring new employees. In fact, those of you who have read my book, *Swan's How to Pick the Right People Program* (John Wiley & Sons, 1989), or been through my "How to Pick the Right People" selection interview workshop will recognize the three categories I'm about to discuss. They're useful for determining the job requirements when you're preparing to interview a job candidate. They're just as useful as a source of performance factors. They represent the totality of any job, in a way that transcends the more obvious factors which are usually covered by a job description.

Knowledge, Skills, and Abilities

The first category represents what human resource professionals call the "KSAs": the "knowledge, skills, and abilities" necessary for success. Exactly what knowledge base, what sorts of presentation skills, what kind of verbal or analytical skills are necessary? What level of technical knowledge, territory management exposure, or product knowledge is needed by an incumbent in this job? What do they have to know to be successful and—because in the context of the performance appraisal this is an ongoing process—are they keeping their knowledge current?

Knowledge, skills, and abilities thus represent one arena from which one might select the job requirements that will become performance factors; these are the things managers first think of when they think of an individual's competence, and they're the performance factors that are the most specific to an individual job—the least likely to apply to all the organization's employees. As performance factors the KSAs are very useful in pinpointing easy-to-repair deficits in performance. If "effective presentation skills" is a performance factor and a manager discovers that an employee has a weakness in this area, that diagnosis can be a fruitful springboard for a developmental plan.

Behaviors

The second arena includes qualities that are subtle and harder to define and which are often thought of as personality traits: things such as "initiative," "motivation," "stick-to-it-iveness," and "reliability." Think of them as behaviors, not traits, to underline the fact that, for the performance appraisal and selection interview, they should be defined in a way that makes them clearly measurable. How would an employee have to behave to *show* the "initiative" or "stick-to-it-itiveness" needed on this job?

Managers often have wildly different definitions of these words. That doesn't mean, however, that they don't describe realities which are important for high quality job performance. It just means that in order for these words to be useful there must be general agreement among managers on what the words mean in relation to a given job—and of course that message must be clearly communicated to the employee.

What do I as a manager mean by initiative: Do I want my employees to show some degree of independence, that is, that when I suggest an idea they give me their point of view? Very good. That's not the same as the initiative they might display by launching a project of their own without asking. Perhaps some managers would applaud one kind of initiative but wouldn't want to encourage the other. These managers should be sure to define the term, both for themselves and for the employee.

An organization might feel that "a positive response to direction and authority" is vital for employees at a certain level. By this I mean that after the employees have given their opinion or input, and once the manager has decided how to proceed, employees execute the plan without giving an argument. Organizations don't want a "yes" person, but they don't want someone who will sit there debating with management forever. That's a distinction all participants should be aware of so they can shoot for the right target.

Environmental Factors

The third arena or aspect of any job is the environment in which employees have to work. Often this includes facts management is reluctant to acknowledge, but of which everyone who works at an organization or in a particular division or department is tacitly aware. If an ability and willingness to cope with these realities is necessary for high quality and productivity, they should be faced when you're drawing up the performance factors. Do employees have to deal with deadline pressure? Do they have to show political savvy and tact when coping with arbitrariness and capriciousness? Or perhaps you are in the financial services industry, where ethics and confidentiality have been recently reinforced as important values. If so, that aim can and should be spelled out in the performance factors.

It isn't likely that a hundred skills, behaviors, or environmental factors are important enough to the job or to the organization to be made into standard performance factors. Chances are that two or three from each category will serve, yielding eight to fifteen performance factors.

In an ideal performance management program there would probably be a core group of performance factors that express values important to the organization as whole, and which would therefore be part of the performance appraisal for every job: others, especially skills, but also some performance factors drawn from job-relevant behaviors and environmental factors, would be different for each job or job-family.

HOW TO MEASURE PERFORMANCE FACTORS

While performance objectives are usually either met or not, performance factors aren't as cut and dried. Therefore any performance factors arrived at must include some way of recording gradations of performance. Repellent as some of us may find it, a time comes when we just can't escape making an evaluative judgment. It is a process we have grown accustomed to from school—A, B, C, D or F, and most people continue, in every area of life, to be evaluated according to some sort of scale; and with remarkable regularity, it turns out to be a five point scale (the ABCDF of our early schooling was a five point scale).

There are actually sound reasons for this. For one thing, whenever a three point scale (say, outstanding, satisfactory, unsatisfactory) is established for almost any kind of test, it almost immediately becomes a five point scale. Somehow, raters cannot resist putting notches between the three points— too many employees turn out to be a little better than satisfactory but not quite outstanding, a little less than satisfactory but not quite unsatisfactory. Because three point scales become five point scales anyway, we might as well start them out that way.

On the other hand, a scale of more than five points makes an implicit claim to precision which it is hard to justify unless relying solely on easily quantifiable objective evidence such as sales figures or numbers of widgits produced per hour: it's really not appropriate for the evaluation of performance factors or performance objectives. A five point scale is perceived by most people as reasonable.

You'll notice, however, that on the form I've presented at the end of Chapter Four, the ratings are not associated with letters or numbers. The scale for performance factors may translate into numbers as manager eventually reaches for an overall rating on the employee. But for purposes of discussion between manager and the employee, it's better to avoid numbers or letters. The manager doesn't want to reduce the employee to a number. He or she doesn't want to encourage the employee to think of it as a grade, but to focus on performance. The words are better. They draw attention from the grade to its meaning.

> *greatly exceeded the standard*
> *exceeded the standard*
> *met the standard*
> *did not meet the standard*
> *significantly below the standard*

Note that the use of the scale makes it necessary for the manager to know what level of performance is associated with each. So not only does the manager have to know what he or she means (and what the organization means) by the term "initiative"; but he or she ought to know what an employee must do to exceed the standard set and what behavior would fall short of it.

A definition of "initiative" might go like this: "Well, I expect that if you tell me about a problem, you also present a solution or options. If in fact you've thought it through and given me three options, one of which you recommend—and it's a reasonable solution, not an impossible solution—then you've met the standard. If you solve the problem before you get to me, that's even better; that would be *exceeding* the standard. If you present me problems without solutions than you're at the bottom of the scale; if you give me solutions that aren't workable then I would put you one up from the bottom."

By the way, managers should think carefully about the distance between the midpoint of the scale and "occasionally exceeds" or "consistently exceeds." There's a temptation to see the list as representing a scale ascending and descending in equal increments, but this may not reflect the reality of the job. For example, if having met the standard means the employee should get at least ten of the 12 monthly reports in on the due date and two no more than one week late, that would be the standard. However, "occasionally exceeds the standard" isn't necessarily getting 11 on time and one late. Achieving 11 might represent such a Herculean effort that it would more justly represent "consistently exceeded the standard." As for "occasionally did not meet the standard," that might not mean getting nine reports in on time, but some other number depending upon the degree of difficulty of that task.

If you've ever taken a course in negotiation skills you may be familiar with this kind of thinking. Suppose someone says to you, "I'll offer you $120,000 for your house" and you say, "No, I want $150,000" and they say, "OK, I'd like to make this deal work,

I'll offer you $125,000." Well, your next bid need not be $145,000—it could be $149,000. Just because the party you're negotiating with went up five thousand doesn't mean you have to go down the same amount. Yet that's what people often do out of a blind love of symmetry.

The same logic applies to the standards used for the performance factors. They should be fair, of course; they should reflect the realities of the job; and they should be consistent from employee to employee; but they needn't be symmetrical. In fact, it is more likely that a geometric relationship exists for the different levels of performance.

CHAPTER SEVEN

Creating an Employee Development Plan

The performance plan, covered in previous chapters, focuses on the objectives an employee will be responsible for in the coming year. These are focused activities which move the organization forward. The manager creates them at the beginning of the year, probably at the end of the performance appraisal meeting for the previous year, and (together with the performance factors) they become Part I and II of the performance appraisal form for next year—a portion of the "report card" section of the form. However, it's only one half of the total plan for the year.

The Employee Development Plan (Figure 7.1) is the second half of the plan for next year. As I mentioned in Chapter Four, progress in meeting the employee development plan is not formally or directly rated or included in the overall summary of performance rating (Part III of the form). Yet achievement (or lack of it) of the development plan

DEVELOPMENT PLAN
(OBJECTIVES)

- TO IMPROVE PERFORMANCE IN CURRENT JOB

- TO PREPARE FOR ADVANCEMENT OPPORTUNITIES,
  CAREER ADVANCEMENT OR GROWTH

- TO ENRICH THE EMPLOYEE'S EXPERIENCE
  OF THE ON-GOING JOB

FIGURE 7.1 The three options for an Employee Development Plan.

indirectly affects the evaluations and ratings the manager arrives at in Part I and Part II — by helping employees improve, in the long run it helps them achieve higher standards. The employee development plan is a means of applying the information gathered in the evaluative sections of the appraisal, and it concerns what many managers consider the most useful application of the performance management process: developing employees, either to bring them up to speed in their current job, or to give them the skills needed to advance them to positions of greater responsibility. If advancement is not an option, or of no interest to the employee, the development plan can at least be used to enrich the employee's experience on the job on a daily basis.

Having said this much, I will grant you that this criterion may not make sense for every employee in every job. Some employees may be so focused, some jobs may be so routine, that there simply isn't any room for change, and to require it would be unrealistic, but surely those are the minority. For most people in most jobs there's room for improvement or enrichment of the every day experience even if advancement were not available as an option — at the very least, there's usually room for expanded responsibilities within the framework of the existing job.

IMPROVING PERFORMANCE IN CURRENT JOB

It's only rational that before you start talking with an employee about how they can advance in their career or expand their responsibilities, the primary issue should be helping them meet the standard in their current job. Of course this does not mean that advancement can't be used as an incentive even for employees who aren't up to speed. The manager can simply say, "Let's get these problem solved first, then we'll talk about preparing for promotion or job enrichment."

Even if an employee's performance is satisfactory, the appraisal will probably uncover areas which can be strengthened. New or inexperienced employees are not likely to meet performance standards immediately, and even for more experienced employees, perfection is rare. There's usually something that could be improved.

Applying the appraisal immediately to the task of improving employee performance takes some of the sting out for those employees who haven't performed up to the set standards. The development plan makes it clear that the appraisal isn't just an excuse to eliminate or lower salary increases or bonuses. It's being used to solve problems—that's underlined by the fact that the same form that's used to identify the performance problem is used for the employee development plan.

ADVANCEMENT OR ENRICHMENT

But a development plan can do more than improve current performance. For employees who show potential, the appraisal can be the basis for a development plan that prepares them for advancement to another level or role. For those managers who are

in a position to offer it, the possibility of advancement is often an effective motivator and a reward
for successful performance.

On the other hand, the timing, the nature of your
organization, or the nature of the particular jobs may
make advancement to a new position unlikely; or this
particular employee may not be interested in advancement. What do you then? What can you offer
employees who are performing well in their current
job?

Well, just because you can't give somebody a promotion doesn't mean you can't create a meaningful
development plan. A manager can still ask the employee: "What would you like to learn? What additional skills would you like to acquire? What can we
do to prepare you in the event there ever were an
opportunity? Are there tasks you're responsible for
that you'd like to do even better? Are there things
you'd like to do or learn even though it isn't directly
or formally part of your job?"

By mentoring, by giving them exposure to another
area or activity, or by letting them take charge on
a day when you're not there, you can enrich their
experience so that they feel like an important and
valued part of the team. That sort of development
plan might be possible even when advancement is
not an option, and it can help keep employees' interest and enthusiasm alive.

DEVELOPMENTAL OBJECTIVES

In practice, the developmental plan will consist of a
set of developmental objectives. The same objective
setting procedures used for the performance plan
are used for this purpose: they give employees something to shoot for, and give both parties a way to
measure progress.

If there were performance objectives not met or performance factors rated below standard in the "report card" phase of the performance appraisal, the manager should create with the employee developmental objectives that would address those issues. If the employee is not meeting expectations in several areas, the entire development plan may consist of these types of objectives. In most cases, however, employees would also have developmental objectives to prepare them for advancement or enrich their experience on the job; in the absence of the need to improve on their current job, the manager can concentrate all their efforts on advancement or enrichment.

How would a manager arrive at development objectives? In the course of the assessment of the employee's performance and the discussion with the employee, the manager should try to determine why a particular objective was not met (or why the employee did not "consistently meet the expectation" for a particular performance factor). In doing so the manager may identify a skill or knowledge deficit which needs to be addressed and think of a development objective that will target that problem.

You may remember that in the chapter on performance objectives I said they should be set in a way that requires "stretch." With developmental objectives, the case for "stretching" is even clearer. A developmental objective can be like an exercise; it can be like pumping iron, if you will. You don't go from pressing 20 pounds directly to pressing 100 pounds unless you want to wind up in the hands of a chiropractor. That would be unrealistic. But you don't want to stay at 20 pounds forever, either. That wouldn't get you anywhere. If employees are to develop and grow they must be set tasks that require some effort, that go a little beyond what they've done before. A good manager will set goals that are exciting, that require employees to learn a bit and to expand their skills or knowledge.

One way of improving performance—the first that occurs to most managers—is formal training. This can take a number of different forms which are all worth considering. Perhaps your organization offers internal training programs which may be applicable. There may be things the employee can do right within the department that qualify as on-the-job training; there's self-paced learning with the aid of audio cassettes, video cassettes, or books. And of course, if your organization is willing to foot the bill, sending the employee to appropriate outside courses can be very worthwhile. Any of these training options can become a developmental objective.

However, it's a mistake to regard training as the only or primary solution to performance problems. It's an understandable mistake, and it's understandable that training should be the first thing most of us think of when it comes to employee development—it's a solution specifically designed for the problem. It takes the matter out of our hands; it's a neat package. I know of one manager who's solution to developing an employee was simply to scan a list of outside management courses and pick one or two that the employee should attend: voila, the employee development plan.

The problem is that many performance problems are either not susceptible to training per se or training is not the most efficient or effective solution. It may be that mentoring and ongoing coaching and counseling during the course of the year would be more productive. If, when a particular problematic situation issue comes up, the manager would help the employee think it through, eventually he or she would be able to think it through alone.

For example, suppose Susan must periodically do presentations to another department. On her performance review for last year she is rated as not meeting the expectations level for the performance factor which includes this activity. While discussing last year's appraisal, Susan and her manager agree that her presentations suffer from her tendency not to get all her information organized prior to the presentation. They also decide that over the next three months she'll meet with her manager prior to those presentations, and he'll help her think through her presentation and anticipate objections and problems. The manager could then set the developmental objective to include the expectation that at the end of the three-month period Susan would be able to do it herself. The developmental objective would read: "For the next three months, Susan will meet with me one day prior to each weekly presentation to the purchasing department; at the end of the three-month period Susan is expected to demonstrate that she can on her own anticipate problems or objections and develop strategies for dealing with them."

In the above circumstances this objective was part of the "improvement in current job" aspect of the development plan, but such presentations could represent an opportunity to develop a skill necessary for success in the next position for which Susan may become eligible.

Another example is a situation in which Bob has been rated "occasionally met the standard" on the performance factor "quality of work." In the context of his job that means that he submits reports with typos, and the developmental objective might be that prior to submitting any document Bob would use the word processor's spell check procedure and proofread it himself prior to submission; he would be deemed to have met the objective if, over the entire next appraisal period, no more than every fifth document has any typos.

SOURCES OF DEVELOPMENTAL OBJECTIVES

Where do developmental objectives come from? You look first, of course, at what is wrong. If there are large areas in which performance is not up to standard, then 100 percent of the developmental objectives might come from performance factors and performance objectives. If a manager is mainly concentrating on advancement or enrichment, then all the sources which provide performance objectives would also apply to developmental objectives. In cases clearly leading toward promotion, the manager could use the performance appraisal objectives and performance factors for employees at *the next level up* as a source of developmental objectives.

GUIDELINES OF THE EMPLOYEE DEVELOPMENT PLAN

Involve the Employee

While the whole appraisal should involve the employee and have employee commitment to the performance objectives, it's even more vital that the development plan be created with the employee. The developmental objectives must emerge from a process of negotiation. Presenting it as a fait accompli will result in much less commitment and cooperation. If a manager can demonstrate through a well-documented appraisal that there is a need for improvement, it's reasonable to ask that employees take some responsibility for their own growth.

Consider Improving Performance on Current Job First

Past performance objectives not met, and performance factors rated below standard are the first sources of the developmental objectives.

Obtain Dual Acceptance/Acknowledgment of Developmental Needs

A manager needs the employee's cooperation, so the first necessity for a development plan is that employees accept the fact that development is needed. That's one reason why it's so important to have a performance appraisal method that carries a conviction of fairness and clearly sets common standards for different employees. Then, if an employee says, "Well, I think I worked as hard as I could on that issue," the manager can say, "Well, you remember at the beginning of the year we set the targets, I said this is what we need. Everyone else around you is easily able to meet that standard or better, so I think it's a reasonable standard to hold you to."

With the development plan, a manager is also saying, "I'm willing to develop a plan with you to help you improve in this area. If you feel that you can work on it on your own, fine. But remember, if you perform at that same level next year you'll get "occasionally met the standard" on that performance factor just as you did this year. But if you want to do better I'd like to help."

Put Developmental Objectives in Writing

Even though these developmental objectives are an "off the record" part of the performance appraisal in the sense that the employee is not directly rated on them, some managers resist the idea of even going that far and actually putting them in writing. Deeply embedded in the corporate culture of many organizations is the following philosophy: "Let's talk informally, but let's not write everything down, because we don't want it on the record." This implies that things that go into the record are negative. But take into account that what can go in the record is a *plan*. Simply: here's where we are, here's where we'd like to be. Here are the areas in which the employee didn't do as well as we would have liked; here are the areas in which he or she did do well. Let's see if we can augment these, and do even better in those satisfactory areas and improve performance in the weak areas.

An Employee Who Doesn't Want to Advance

What about an employee who is performing up to standards, but *isn't* interested in growing (not even in the sense of "enrichment" we discussed earlier). Is it worth it to spend the time and energy even to do a performance appraisal, let alone attempt a development discussion with that individual? I think it is. For one thing, as a manager I would still want to maintain my employees current satisfactory level of performance.

Let's take the extreme. Let's suppose we do not bother to do a development plan for John, who is meeting the standard and has no apparent desire for promotion or enrichment. Why bother? Why bother talking to him about his performance, why bother even giving him a written appraisal? Nothing has changed about John, so there's no need to do it, and (assuming I had the administrative authority to do so) I skip him this year.

Well, I would argue that as a result of this well-meant neglect, John's interest might decline, and even his performance might decline, because my message to John is that I have forgotten about him. Just to maintain performance at current levels it helps to speak to employees formally, to give them positive reinforcement. It helps to remind them that I know how well they're doing and to prove that I am paying attention by referring to specific instances during the course of the year. "John, over this year I noticed several instances in which you caught some small errors that could have led to serious problems. I want to let you know that I noticed, and I want you to know I appreciate your continued attention to details, and I've made a note on your performance appraisal about this."

That kind of feedback can be helpful even if it doesn't affect the employee's actual rating. Also, remember, people are full of surprises. It's conceivable that when the time of the performance appraisal discussion comes, even old dependable John will turn out to have some things he'd like to learn about or skills he'd like to develop, things no one ever would have considered.

Obviously, though, if there has been no change from last year's perfectly satisfactory performance, a little reinforcement to maintain John's behavior via a briefer, less complex discussion would be in order.

CHAPTER EIGHT

How to Make Your Organization's System Work

In the preceding chapters I've presented the performance management program I believe represents the best balance of elements to ensure a fair and accurate performance appraisal, a program which puts the performance appraisal to the best use and wins cooperation and commitment from employees. It's the program I recommend you apply if you can.

But what if you aren't free to do whatever you want? As I said in Chapter One, most managers are asked to implement a performance appraisal system which they receive as a fait accompli from those higher up the totem pole. How can you apply the lessons I've presented so far? Can you play by the rules your organization has laid down for the performance appraisal and at the same time conduct a performance management program that gives you the benefits I've described earlier in the book?

Fortunately, in most cases you can. Most organization's performance appraisal systems are either similar in form to the one in this book (perhaps giving different names to the various elements) or contain one element among the several presented here; and usually, the manager has a great deal of latitude in applying the performance appraisal. One might generalize and say the more inadequate and haphazard the system, the more latitude you are probably given in applying it: if your organization uses behaviorally anchored rating scales, with its elaborate apparatus, you probably don't have much leeway in how you use it; but on the other hand, you've probably received detailed instructions.

If your organization's performance appraisal system is inadequate to the tasks it must perform, the chances are you have room to take action to repair the faults in the system. Where the criteria for the appraisal are lax, vague, or insufficiently job-related, you can use those criteria, but define them for yourself in a concrete, job-related way. When the formal components of the performance appraisal are in your opinion inadequate for your purposes, you can supplement them with other informal elements—informal in the sense that they may not fit on the form you send to your human resources department, but would be communicated manager to employee. In fact, actually attaching additional documentation to a performance appraisal form is rarely a problem.

IF YOUR ORGANIZATION'S SYSTEM ONLY COVERS PERFORMANCE FACTORS

For example, in many organizations the performance appraisal consists entirely of a list of traits or behaviors—roughly corresponding to the performance factors introduced in Chapter Six of this book for which top management supplies no definition or standard. To shape this performance appraisal into one more useful for your purposes you might use two basic strategies:

- Define the traits in a more job relevant fashion
- Give your employees informal performance objectives

Define the Traits in a More Concrete Fashion

Energy, motivation, initiative, cooperation—what's wrong with a manager wanting these qualities in his or her employees? Nothing, providing the manager is able to define them in a concrete job-relevant way.

To be defendable as fair performance appraisal criteria, to lead to better performance instead of pointless misunderstandings, traits and behaviors should be given definitions that are specific. That way employees will know what is really being said and what they need to do to meet the standard.

To be really useful these definitions should relate as specifically as possible to the actual requirements of the particular job—every employee in the organization may be expected to show "initiative" if that's a value your organization prizes, but clearly "initiative" is going to mean one thing for a vice president and another for a shop foreman. That difference should be made explicit.

Your organization may not have any guidelines closely defining the traits in its laundry list of personal qualities or behaviors expected of employees, but that doesn't prevent you from having a concrete definition of your own for each trait. All it requires is a little research and a little thinking, relating each trait to the job in question. Ask people who know something about the job—the employees themselves, managers who supervise that position, people who interface with that job, and ask yourself—what is meant by each term with respect to that particular position.

The variety of meanings different people attach to a phrase like "demonstrates high energy" might surprise you. Manager A might say: "What I mean by that is, you have to be able to juggle six things in the air at once, shift back and forth from one to the other throughout the day. You have to do it without resenting it, resisting it, without being exhausted by it, because that's the job."

That's quite different from Manager B who tells her employees, "I don't know, it seems like you weren't really working at your full effort, you don't have enough energy on a daily basis." That's too vague. But perhaps what Manager B really means is this: "At ten thirty at night, I want you to be just as detail oriented and just as focused and just as accurate as you are at seven in the morning. That's what I'm expecting of you. It needs to be done and done correctly even though you've had a long hard day."

Employees in the accounting area, finance area, or systems area may have to come in at 7:30 in the morning and begin immediately doing critical detailed activities: they may need to be sharp from the moment they begin. Their supervisor might legitimately tell them, "That's what I mean by high energy, not just high motor activity. I need you to be attentive to detail and accurate even when you're tired."

Some employees in systems and data processing departments are "on call" over the weekend. When the system goes down, they get a call on their beeper, and they have to be on the phone within five minutes. If that call comes at four o'clock in the morning, they have to quickly get the cobwebs out of their mind and give concrete, specific answers because things are going downhill fast! If that's part of Larry's job, it can be part of the description of "energy" for his performance appraisal; you can make it clear to Larry at the beginning of the appraisal period that that is what is expected of him, and (perhaps along with other concretely defined behaviors) will represent the standard for the issue of "energy" on his performance appraisal. If routinely, or even a few times, he was called over the weekend and wasn't available for fifteen or twenty minutes or said, "Oh, I'll call you back, let me get up and get a cup of coffee" this would be below the standard of performance set for "energy."

That's quite different from saying, "I don't know, you're just not—there've been a bunch of incidents, I can't be specific—I just don't think you're responsible."

Take that universally desired quality I mentioned earlier: "initiative." Many organizations use the term without defining it very clearly. This needn't remain a vague, subjective quality. It can be defined so concretely that no employee need be in doubt as to what behavior will result in a rating of "having met the standard." A manager can say to an employee, "Terry, this is what I mean by initiative: inevitably you're going to come to me with problems. But I also want you to bring three possible solutions when you come and indicate which one you recommend and why. That's what I mean by 'initiative' on the performance factor list."

With that clear cut definition, at the end of the year a manager can tell his or her employee, "Look, I've got information here from data I gathered over the entire appraisal period. You came to me with about a dozen problems, things you ought to have brought to me. But for half of them, you just pre-sented me the problem and you left it in my lap. Remember our goal at the beginning was that when you come to me I need those possible solutions as well. We discussed this several times during the year as the incidents occurred. As a result, I'm forced to rate you as 'not meeting the standard' for this performance factor."

That's much different from saying, "Terry, I don't know, you're just not showing enough initiative"— which may be what all the managers in your orga-nization are saying based on the simple list of qual-ities on which your organization rates its employees. If you approach it properly, you can make that list of qualities clear, fair, and of use to you.

By the way, in addition to defining the qualities more concretely you should first review the list to make sure it's comprehensive—that it includes all the qualities for which you want to hold your or-ganization responsible. You may want to add to that list. Those additional items may or may not become an official part of the performance appraisal, de-pending on your organization's policies and how much latitude you are given.

Your organization should give specific meaning to the rating system it attaches to the qualities. Sup-posing the rating system consists of a simple one to five scale on each quality, without defining what the points on the scale mean. The manager should focus on the score or the number that tell the employee: "If you meet the standard we agreed to, you will be rated at the midpoint of the scale; if you sometimes exceed the standard, you will be rated up one level; if you sometimes fall below the standard . . . ," and so on. Then you can go even further to define more exactly what behavior exceeds or falls short of the standard.

Give Employees Informal
Performance Objectives

Regardless of the appraisal system you're using, the analysis of the job which forms the basis for the performance management program presented in this book still applies: one facet of the employee's job consists of the formal or informal objectives, goals, assignments, or expectations for that person; the other aspect of the job is *how* the employee achieves those goals, and the ongoing behaviors that characterize his or her working methods.

If your organization's form only deals with performance factors or their equivalent, the limitations of that form need not prevent balanced and effective performance reviews. While the form does not mention performance objectives, the manager can set three to five goals or expectations that he or she has for the employee over the next year or review period and hold them accountable for it. If he or she intends to do this, the manager should coordinate with the human resources department to make sure there are no objections and to get approval for doing it.

The manager and the employee may realize that the only thing that's going to be submitted is the simple little form that the organization sponsors. That's what's official. However, that should not prevent the manager from working with the employees in a more sophisticated way. After all, the performance appraisal is not the only means of influencing employees, and a manager has other uses for the appraisal than just to supply the human resources department with a set of numbers. Performance objectives can be used to *manage* the employees, even if not officially to appraise them. And in fact, many managers go far beyond what is asked of them on the performance appraisal form and add all kinds of additional and relevant information on their employees' performance: they attach memos or additional narrative information, additional documentation. They are on pretty safe ground doing this as long as what they hand in is job-relevant and can be documented.

Whatever your organization's system, a good manager can maintain ongoing rigors and objectives and goals with employees by imposing correct procedures on an inadequate system.

WHAT IF YOUR ORGANIZATION'S SYSTEM INCLUDES OBJECTIVES BUT NOT PERFORMANCE FACTORS?

The performance appraisal form of some organizations consists of a piece of paper that says "Objectives" in one column and "Results" in another. If you have a system which includes objectives but not performance factors you will recognize that it's one thing for a manager to evaluate them on whether or not they met their objective, but *how* they met their objective is still an important issue—that's one of the issues that performance factors were meant to address.

For example, suppose the employees met objective number three, but they did it in a way which alienated individuals in another department and gaining cooperation for future projects is jeopardized? The employees need to get feedback—and the manager has a right to let them know that how they achieve their objectives is important and will be included in the evaluation. Otherwise, next year they could say, "Well I met my objective again; you never said you were evaluating how I did it." Therefore, on that "Results" column the manager *should* indicate any qualifying issues regarding how those objectives were met.

It's not critical that you have a part of the form called "Performance Factors" and another part called "Performance Objectives." The important thing is to make sure that both these components of the job are reflected in your appraisal.

WHAT IF YOUR ORGANIZATION USES THE "GLOBAL ESSAY" SYSTEM

If your organization uses the "global essay" form of the performance appraisal (see Chapter Two), then, almost by definition anything goes—the manager has complete latitude to apply every suggestion I've given in this book. A global essay approach by definition leaves everything up to the manager: to assign employees performance factors and performance objectives at the beginning of the year; to explain how they work; to monitor and coach during the year on these issues, and so on. The manager can even make it official by explaining the process in the essay section: such a global essay will be fair, rational, and defendable in court, even if those of other managers in your organization are not.

WHEN YOUR PERFORMANCE APPRAISAL PROGRAM CHANGES COURSE

An interesting question that comes up in my seminars occasionally, is this: "OK, Bill, suppose we take your advice and from this year on we set performance objectives, and define standards of performance on the performance factors, and base the performance appraisal on data we collect throughout the year. There's bound to be a sudden change in many of our employees' ratings based on this change in our procedures. How do we deal with that?"

Well, to take this objection to it's logical conclusion, what's the alternative? Would you continue to rate employee's inaccurately so as not to create a discrepancy between this year's rating and last year's? Of course not. At some point it is necessary to wake up and say: "I haven't been as organized and clear as I could have these past couple years regarding the performance appraisal process, but here's how we're going to proceed this coming year."

All a manager can do is be clear and candid, and give employees fair warning of the new approach. This year, when the manager sits down with your employee, it's the beginning a new cycle. He or she would say, "It's clear to me that last year my ratings were based mostly on what happened the last two months of the year (or whatever went wrong). This year will be different. Together we're going to develop the plan for next year and I'm going to make crystal clear what I'm expecting of you. I can tell you exactly what you need to do for you to get an overall rating that meets the standard or exceeds it."

If the employees are sharp, they will recognize that the game plan has changed and they're going to be held more accountable for their actions than they have been before. It's like getting a new English teacher who says at the beginning of the year: "You're going to have three book reports and if they're not in by the date they're due you automatically drop by one letter grade . . ." And they will think, "I did pretty well in my previous English class without working very hard, but I can see that in this class it's going to require more attention on my part."

It is doubtful that any of upper management would

run to the manager and say, "What's going on here? You rated this person for the last three years as 'exceptional' and now you're saying they 'met the standard.' " But if they do, the answer is the same. "I have made improvements in my performance appraisal system—the sudden change in the ratings is due to a sudden increase in accuracy."

CHAPTER NINE

Writing the Appraisal

The pages that follow introduce a "Performance Rating Analysis Worksheet" that fits my program; it explains in detail how to rate employees on each performance factor and performance objective, and how to resolve or summarize the whole appraisal into a level of achievement statement number which will represent the employee's overall rating for the year.

When I speak of "writing the appraisal," however, I'm not referring merely to the clerical exercise of checking off boxes and averaging numbers, but also the crucial business of arriving at sound judgments based on the evidence accumulated over the entire appraisal period. It's a task that requires the manager to be as fair and objective as possible, and for most people, there's the rub. If you're a human being and not a robot all your judgments are to some degree subjective. If there's no one to contradict your judgment it's that much harder to know when you're wrong.

COMMON RATING ERRORS

In an effort to cope with this problem, industrial psychologists interested in how ratings are done in the performance appraisal have categorized the most common rating errors. As you read through them, think about which you may have observed or of which you may yourself have been a victim.

1. Similar to Me—Tending to rate people higher if they are similar to you (have the same values, interests likes), or rating them lower if they are not similar to you.

   While this may sound like the behavior of snobs and aristocrats, it continues to be a serious problem in a workforce characterized by increasing diversity, in which some managers cannot relate to the cultural differences of their employees.

2. Positive Lenience—Rating higher than a person deserves. "I give high ratings. It motivates my employees, it makes them feel good." Particularly strong tendency if rater is rushed.

   This usually takes the form of giving Bob a higher rating than he deserves, so as not to discourage him, hoping he'll do better next year. However, when Mark and Susan, who work here too receive the rating they deserve, see Bob doing as well as them in the ratings, the effect on them is demoralizing and discouraging. And what do you do next year when Bob *doesn't* improve? He can argue that his performance didn't change from last year, so why should he get a lower rating? In fact being rated higher than one deserves is demotivating and fosters disrespect for the process.

3. Negative Leniency—Being reluctant to assign high ratings to individuals. Rating people lower than they deserve. "Nobody's perfect." Another strong tendency if rater is rushed.

   Some managers set goals and objectives that are unattainable to begin with so high ratings are never possible. Others are "strict graders" and refuse to ever give a rating at the top of the scale.

4. Halo/Horns Effect—Being overly influenced by a single favorable or unfavorable trait, which colors the judgment of the individual's other traits. Alternatively, allowing another person's positive or negative evaluation prior to the manager's review to unduly affect the rating of the employee.

   Jeff had an incredible success in the past. Now it seems that he can do no wrong. Conversely, Jeanne had an off year two years ago. Her current high quality performance is diminished by the memory of two years ago.

5. Recency Effect—Rating someone down or up based solely on recent events. Ignoring the performance of the entire period. "What have you done for me lately?"

   This is especially likely when the manager hasn't been keeping records during the year. Recent behavior and performance seems more relevant and meaningful, even if we remember the earlier performance.

6. Attribution Bias—Tending to see poor performance more within the control of the individual, and to see superior performance as more influenced by external factors.

   This sounds rather academic at first glance, but you are probably quite familiar with it. "If Steve is successful it's because of me. If not, it's his fault." Of course perhaps I didn't coach him enough or set clear enough goals or check back often enough.

7. Stereotyping—Generalizing across a group. Not recognizing individual differences.

   Beyond the obvious gender, racial, or cultural assumptions, sometimes made, I run across managers who assume all engineers can learn quickly, all R&D scientists are highly analytical and all sales persons are motivated and ambitious.

8. Contrast Effect—Making comparisons. Evaluating the employee relative to the person last evaluated.

   This is most obviously seen with teachers or professors who rip to shreds the first student's paper, only to realize by the fourth or fifth that every student seems to be missing the point: all the papers that come *after* that realization are treated much more leniently.

9. First Impression—Forming an initial positive or negative judgment and then ignoring or distorting subsequent information to avoid changing the initial impression.

   While similar to the Halo/Horns effect, here the rater actually is unable to shake an initial impression or admit a mistaken perception. This phenomenon has caused many a personal relationship to drag on longer than the "objective evidence" would support.

10. Central Tendency—Placing people in the middle of the scale, or close to the midpoint to avoid extreme positions. Playing safe.

    Some organizations have actually forced managers to make this error by requiring a forced distribution or rating across employees to resolve a clustering of ratings at the top of the scale. Grade inflation should be corrected, but forced distribution is a draconian solution.

There's no way to entirely eliminate the subjective element from judgments about employee performance. If a manager has a mountain of facts at his or her disposal, chances of being objective are greater than if the manager has only a few. But managers still have to interpret those facts and decide which facts are the most meaningful.

Nevertheless, it's safe to say that good documentation and a systematic approach can make the manager right a much greater percentage of the time. At the very least, it can make all his or her decisions defendable: the facts and procedures prove that judgments were not made arbitrarily. For that matter, systematic documentation and evaluation also offers other people the opportunity of looking at that same data and coming to their own conclusions, which can be important if upper management's input and approval is required.

In this chapter I'm going to talk about writing the appraisal as if you were using the performance management program I've presented in Chapters Four through Seven. I think you'll find it useful, though, even if you can't employ all the steps in my version of the performance appraisal. I think you'll find that the principles of writing an accurate and effective performance appraisal are the same whatever appraisal methods you use.

It's really a three step process.

1. Gather and Analyze Data Throughout Appraisal Period
2. Rate the Performance
3. Write the Narrative Portions of the Appraisal

Of these three tasks, the first is by far the most time consuming and complex. It's also the most crucial.

GATHER AND ANALYZE DATA THROUGHOUT APPRAISAL PERIOD

If a manager wants to avoid the "recency effect" among other common errors, this is really the only way. Yet for many supervisors it seems to be the most difficult to square with the realities of every day management. "Where do I find the time?" Much depends on the degree of contact between manager and employees. How often does the manager really see the employees doing what they do?

Because it is so complex, I'm going to cover this subject in considerable detail here.

Collect Data at Regular Intervals

The manager must determine in advance the time frame within which data will be collected throughout the appraisal period—and then, when the time comes, do it. You might think of these as periodic "sub-appraisals," though the manager is not coming to final conclusions; remember, only collecting information and using it for ongoing coaching and feedback.

The period of time that's appropriate for some may be weekly, for others monthly, quarterly or semi-annually, depending on the degree of involvement with the employee and the nature of the employee's responsibilities. Suppose Phil, who is responsible for purchasing, selecting, and installing equipment, and who in addition must maintain the efficiency of the area and achieve these goals through teams reporting to him. The complexity and the high degree of independence inherent in Phil's responsibilities might warrant relatively infrequent "sub-appraisals"— perhaps quarterly. On the other hand, Phil can and should collect information on *his* employees with much greater frequency—their tasks are simpler and more numerous; there's more data to collect.

I believe that most managers are alert to relevant information when it hits their desk. They may even request certain reports or documents regularly. The problem with this approach is that it doesn't insure that they are tracking each objective or performance factor regularly. At the end of the year many gaps exist in the data. I am suggesting a more systematic approach.

Let's assume a manager has decided that a monthly interval is appropriate. At each interval, the manager should see if he or she has information relevant to each of the performance objectives and performance factors. If there isn't, the manager should check over the past month to see if anything has happened that should have been documented that wasn't. If the answer is no, then the manager should pay particular attention in the coming month to collecting data that will fill in the gaps.

Because if by the end of the year there is no information against an objective, how can the manager evaluate it? The goal is to have a number of pieces of information on each objective and performance factor by the end of the appraisal period.

Some managers ask the employee to give them the information relating to the objectives or performance factors in a monthly report. I think that's an excellent idea, but it's not enough by itself. Unless the manager imposes an extremely high degree of organization and structure on it, the report will probably not cover all the performance objectives and all the performance factors; and the manager needs information on all of them. The discipline is to search actively and regularly, throughout the year, for the information on each objective and performance factor.

Do It Openly and Without Pressure

I am not suggesting that a manager stand behind a pole, watch the employees and take notes while they're working. The manager should be able to avoid giving the employees the feeling that they're being watched and judged. He or she should be able to say, "Linda, these are the things we've agreed upon for the next year. We may make some adjustments during the course of the year, but for the moment this is our target. At the end of this year my overall evaluation of your performance will be based on how well you've done on all these individual issues. To assure I have enough information to make that judgment, I'm going to be making notes to myself regarding all these issues on a regular basis. But in addition, there's something you can do to help me. I'd like you to give me information on these issues as they come up, so I'll have accurate information and to help me make a fair assessment at the end of the year."

Is Linda going to run to her manager with every little mistake she makes? Perhaps not. But you'd be surprised how many times an employee who understands the basis for the evaluation will go to the manager and say, "Well, I know you're going to hear about this anyway, but I want to give you my side of it." Or, "Here's something that's happening that isn't going so smoothly, I want to make sure there isn't any misunderstanding regarding the approach I'm about to take." It does add clarity for you to ask for their input. Experience shows that employees are often harsher on themselves than their managers would have been.

Document as You Give Feedback During the Year

If data collected six weeks into the year suggests that employees are veering down the wrong path, it would be unwise to wait until the end of the year to tell them about it: the manager should, if possible, make an intervention right then and there. On the other hand that event, and the action the manager finds necessary to take, should still go into the system as a piece of data for ultimate inclusion in the performance appraisal.

Let's suppose I'm reviewing Linda's performance at the end of the year. She says, "Lately I've been trying hard and doing a lot better. I think I deserve a rating of 'exceeded the standard' on that performance factor." I can say, "In fact, most of the year your performance on that factor 'met the standard' and a couple of times you exceeded it. But in the first two months you were performing 'below the standard' so overall for the year you performed at 'met the standard.' " Certainly it's encouraging that Linda's performance is improving. But the evaluation period is the entire year, not just the last two months.

What Kind of Data Do You Gather?

There are basically three types of information that a manager should gather with reference to employees' performance: objective data, significant incidents and observations.

Objective Data. Only the manager is in a position to know what kinds of objective data are available on the employees. For sales representatives perhaps there are call reports, listings, dollar volume of sales, number of calls per day, or quarterly reports (did the employee get them in on time?). For systems and data processing professionals there may be project milestones or deadlines. For any role there may be quantifiable information that is directly a result of their individual efforts. Whatever objective data exists should be taken into account.

Significant Incidents. These are the same as the "critical incidents" referred to in Chapter Two when we described and analyzed the basic approaches to the performance appraisal. Throughout the year, as they happen, record events that stand out. I call them "significant" instead of "critical" to underline the fact that the manager should not merely be recording negative information. A manager should also record positive events that relate to the performance objectives or performance factors.

The manager may not have many significant incidents on each employee, but even a few can be very informative; and a single significant incident can contain evidence for more than one performance factor or performance objective. For example, suppose mine is a consumer product company: in the middle of the appraisal period, the release date is set for a new product; an advertising campaign is organized and a manufacturing facility is ready to gear up. At the last minute my employee, Alison, discovers that a computer manufacturing software my company planned to supply to the manufacturing group will not be available from the supplier on time. She examines the options: 1) reworking the manufacturing standards; 2) finding another supplier of another program; or 3) arranging for partial shipment. She chooses the third option, which works out well.

That is a complex accomplishment, and it tells a lot about the way Alison works. Through this significant incident she has demonstrated at least some degree of initiative, analytical approach to problem solving, and her command of her technical arena or knowledge. So, for her performance appraisal, that one incident can supply information on all three of those performance factors.

Behaviors You Observe as You Manage

The third category consists of behaviors the manager observes as he or she "manages by walking around," which, by the way, is not a bad approach to management. I pick up a lot of problems about my own company by asking, "Why is that done that way?"

So if while managing by walking around, a manager notices something relevant to performance (not necessarily that the employees are sitting around reading the newspaper), make a note of it.

Have a Record Keeping System

If, on the grounds that it would take too much time, you resisted my suggestion to talk to the employee prior to the performance appraisal, then you're probably saying, "Record keeping system? Here we go again." Record keeping, however, needn't be very elaborate or time-consuming.

If I have just one or two employees, then it might be possible for me to keep my records of employee performance in whatever regular appointment or scheduling book I use: week-at-a-glance, month-at-a-glance or just a daily schedule book.

The situation above is probably an exception, though. Most managers will at some point have to gather data on many individuals at once. They undoubtedly have a file folder on each of those individuals already, thus making record keeping even easier. On a periodic basis, the manager takes the little notes that have accumulated on the employees, date them individually, and dump each into the respective employee's file folder.

By the end of the appraisal period, the manager can open the required file folder and have a number of pieces of paper relevant to that employee's performance. The dating automatically confers a certain order on the collection. Increase the order as the manager separates out all papers that are associated with objective number 1. In other words, the manager would say, "Well, what's my evidence for performance objective number 1?" Not "What do I remember, what do I think of, how do I think they did, do I like them or not?" but "What information do I have?"

If I, as manager, have only two pieces of paper relevant to that objective, I'm in trouble. If I have eight or nine or ten or twelve pieces of paper, plus a critical incident or two, some pieces of observed behavior, several objective pieces of data, perhaps some information I've gotten directly from the employee, I can say with confidence, "Well, obviously the evidence supports the conclusion this person overall is 'meeting the standard' I set," or I can see plenty of evidence that they're way above or way below the standard. Whatever my conclusion may be, the evidence is there.

I'll have that evidence if I throw it into the file folder on a regular basis. If I develop the discipline of making notes to myself on a regular basis and putting them in the file folder, my task at the end of the year will be much easier. In fact, it can take some of the pressure off me during the year, because I know I needn't remember every item relevant to every employee's performance. Once I've made a note to the file I can stop worrying about it.

RATING THE PERFORMANCE

If a manager has gathered information regularly during the year and has a reasonably well-organized record keeping system, he or she is ready to rate the performance on the appraisal form. First the manager will rate each objective, then each performance factor, and finally give an overall or summary rating.

Here are some rules of thumbs for avoiding those common rater errors described at the outset of this chapter.

1. Know the standards
2. Stick to those standards
3. Describe specific facts
4. Document, document, document
5. Use multiple/mini appraisals

Know the Standards

Whether or not the managers are using the formal performance objectives and performance factors that I've put forward in this book, they need to know as precisely as they can what standard they're measuring employees against.

Stick to Those Standards

This is not a restatement of the first rule. Unfortunately, many managers, when they get to this point, throw out the requirements while knowing very well what they are. They say, "Oh, George is doing so well, trying so hard, I think I'll rate him as 'having met the standard' even though, technically, he deserves a 'didn't meet the standard', because, I don't know, I don't want to have an argument with him." Don't do that. If George knows what the standards are and he's been coached well during the year, the final rating shouldn't be a surprise to him. In any case, occasionally presenting reality to an employee is part of a manager's job. Arguments can be avoided by other means than unconditional surrender.

Describe Specific Facts in the Narrative

Probably, several people are going to read this document, including upper management and perhaps one or more individuals in the human resource department. One of the things they're going to look for is whether there is a reasonable correspondence between the narrative and the rating. Another reader of this document will be the employee: making it crystal clear, in the narrative explanation, how the rating was arrived at will greatly reduce the occasions for disagreement or resistance.

Document, Document, Document

This is the performance appraisal equivalent of the "location, location, location" message you will hear if you attend a real estate seminar. With proper documentation ratings are more accurate because the manager has got enough data to reach meaningful conclusions. One might argue over individual facts, but the overall impression is obviously based on the preponderance of evidence.

Not only is this important for the accuracy and defensibility of the appraisal, it's also crucial for employee feedback. Employees' cooperation with plans for problem solving depend on the manager's ability to convince them that problems really exist. Say an employee differs with my conclusion, and I know of seven instances in which the employee failed to meet the standard of performance. The employee might say of one of these instances: "Well, I'm not sure that incident means what you think it means." I can then say, "Okay, let's forget about that one. What about the other six instances? There seems to be a clear pattern here."

Use Multiple/Mini Appraisals

Not all managers have direct contact on a daily basis with each of their employees. There may be someone between them. If so, then that person can give the manager additional data. This middle person should be told what the requirements or standards are, what information they should be looking for. They should gather the information on a weekly or a monthly basis and give it to the manager as part of the overall information gathering process. In organizations that use matrix management, an employee may have four or five managers in the course of a year. In systems and data processing departments and the comptroller/audit department very often a person works on multiple team engagements or assignments, so there are multiple sources of input. All this data can be pooled at the end of the year and used for the performance appraisal.

GIVING GRADES

Throughout this discussion I've tried to persuade you that a manager should not emphasize the numerical score an employee receives with respect to a given performance factor or performance objective: I suggest, in fact, that managers say "met the standard" or "occasionally exceeded the standard" rather than "I've given you a 3" or "I've given you a 4." I believe that's clearly the best approach to use when it comes to managing and improving employee performance.

The fact remains, however, that in order to arrive at an overall rating which will enable a manager to compare different employees' overall performance, or compare a given employee's overall performance this year with his or her overall performance last year, the manager will need to translate these phrases into numbers.

We have now, by the way, reached the point at which most performance appraisal systems fall apart. The overall rating seems to some of us who receive them somehow a mystical interpretation of those individual scores. It's often difficult to arrive at, and still more difficult to defend. But it needn't be, and if you've followed the performance appraisal methods I've presented in this book, I can show you how to arrive at an overall rating that's easy to calculate and meaningful in a way that each participant can easily appreciate.

It all hinges on the issue of weighting. You'll remember that in Chapter Five, "Setting Good Performance Objectives," I mentioned that to give an accurate depiction of the requirements of most jobs a manager must have some way of expressing the relative importance and difficulty of the employee's different responsibilities. Therefore, at the beginning of the appraisal period a manager should assign weights to each of the performance objectives and each of the performance factors. Each is given a certain percentage; all the percentages for the performance objectives add up to one hundred percent, as do the percentages for the performance factors. It's important of course that the manager explain this system clearly to employees, so they understand where to put their greatest efforts, and so the ultimate evaluation doesn't come as a shock.

For example, at the beginning of the year, I told my employee what percentage each of the performance objectives would be worth: perhaps I even negotiated the values with the employee. Of the six objectives: the first objective represented 30%, the second represented 30%, and the remaining four represented 10% each. Those first two objectives, then, represented 60% of the total objectives. If Fred's performance was below standard on those two objectives it's obvious that that fact will weigh heavily on his appraisal even if he achieved perfection with respect to the remaining objectives.

I needn't rely on what is obvious, or on my general sense of how things stack up. Once I've arrived at my decision about the employee's performance on each individual objective, I can calculate the final result at a glance at the Performance Rating Analysis Worksheet (Figure 9.1).

As the form suggests, I'd start by listing the objectives, then under the "Weights" column I'd note the weight that I assigned these objectives with the agreement of the employee, at the beginning of the year. Next I'd circle the rating I've given his performance of the objective. For each objective I'd multiply the weight (that is, the percentage point) times the number representing the rating and note that in the column to the right. I'd add the "Combined" column and divide by 100 to derive my figure for the overall weighted-average rating for objectives.

Then I'd go through the same process for the performance factors; these too can be weighted (though I can of course given them all equal weights if I feel that expresses the truth about the job). This will yield a weighted average rating for performance factors.

Finally, I'd need to repeat the process one final time. If I have decided that Part I (Performance Objectives) and Part II (Performance Factors) are of equal weight, then Part III, the overall summary rating, is a simple average of the two previous

The purpose of this form is to allow you to convert your individual ratings into an overall rating which is meaningful. Use this form three times: once to calculate weighted rating for all objectives, again to calculate weighted rating for all performance factors, and finally to determine the combined weighted rating for objectives and performance factors (Section III of the Model Performance Appraisal Form).

Weight Definitions:

The total number of criteria divided into 100% produces the average weight of each criteria. Adjust the weight for each criteria based upon its level of importance for successful job performance. Be sure the total adds up to 100%.

Rating Definitions:

5 = Performance was clearly exceptional and greatly exceeded expectations

4 = Performance exceeded expectations

3 = Performance met expectations

2 = Performance was minimally acceptable but did not always meet position requirements

1 = Performance was significantly below expectations

Objectives or Performance Factors	Weights	Rating low high	Combined
1. _____	_____	× 1 2 3 4 5 =	_____
2. _____	_____	× 1 2 3 4 5 =	_____
3. _____	_____	× 1 2 3 4 5 =	_____
4. _____	_____	× 1 2 3 4 5 =	_____
5. _____	_____	× 1 2 3 4 5 =	_____
6. _____	_____	× 1 2 3 4 5 =	_____
7. _____	_____	× 1 2 3 4 5 =	_____
8. _____	_____	× 1 2 3 4 5 =	_____

Totals: total W = _____ | Overall rating 1 2 3 4 5 |

must total (100%)   Combined Total

Divide "Combined Total" by 100% for overall rating

FIGURE 9.1 Performance Rating Analysis Worksheet.

weighted averages. If they are weighted unequally (as they usually are) I again multiply the weighted rating for performance objectives and for performance factors against their respective weightings, add the sum and divide by 100. The final number will need to be rounded off to the nearest rating point on my scale.

We might determine that for Bob, his objectives (sales success as shown in dollar volume) represents ninety percent of his job, in which case his performance factors would represent 10%. Basically, barring any unethical behavior, I've decided that I'm less concerned about how he achieved his goals than whether he achieved them. On the other hand, for Brian's job the objectives may represent only 50% of the job; his ongoing day to day behavior is just as important as his objectives.

In both cases, let me repeat, it's important that the employees be fully aware of different weights given their different responsibilities at the beginning of the appraisal period.

When a manager finally comes to the overall rating (Part III of the form) and someone says "Why did you give me this rating?" he or she can say, "Well, this is how I evaluated you on your total objectives; this is how I evaluated you on all your performance factors. Now because, as we've agreed, the objectives were a larger portion of the job, they've been weighted more heavily. Therefore the overall rating for this performance appraisal is that you met the standard." The same logic, and the same explanation, applies when employees question their rating in total performance factors or total performance objectives. "I've rated you as performing above the standard for your last three performance objectives: but you'll remember we agreed that the first objective was as important as the other three combined,

and on that objective you were below the standard—
so on balance I'm rating you as meeting the standard."

This method of rating still requires judgment and
has subjective aspects (it is impossible to entirely
eliminate the subjective element) but it's defendable, reasonable, provides a consistent basis of comparison between employees, and it connects back to
the actual job-relevant events of the year. From the
data gathered throughout the year, a manager will
be able to produce evidence in support of every item.
It's certainly light years away from the usual statement of "it seems to me that overall you're doing
OK, so I've rated you as "meeting the standard."

THE NARRATIVE PORTION OF THE APPRAISAL

The narrative portion of the appraisal is a summary
of the best information collected on each objective
and performance factor. It's the place where managers present their evidence and reasoning for the
conclusions expressed by the rating itself. A manager should write at least one or two sentences of
narrative for each performance objective and performance factor. Below are some rules to remember
when writing a narrative.

Highlight The Best Evidence

For any individual item managers should highlight
their best evidence. If you have ten pieces of information for a particular issue, four or five may be
incontrovertible. Others may leave some room for
interpretation, argument, and discussion. In the
written appraisal managers should highlight the most
defendable evidence or information, saving the rest
for the face to face discussion..

Give Comparison Basis for Qualitative Data

Generally a manager should compare the employee's performance to the standard—not to the performance of any other given individual (i.e., Bob hasn't shown as much energy as Stan). Not only would this create bad feelings when this appraisal is shown to the employee, it's a statistically invalid way of measuring performance. However, a manager can and should point out that the standard for "energy," as defined for that job, is one that the other employees holding the same position in the organization have been easily able to meet or exceed during this appraisal period and in the past. This is an effective way to deal with an employee's contention that the standard is set too high.

Give More Evidence for Especially High and Low Ratings

It's inevitable that upper management and whoever else looks at the performance appraisals, will give closer, more careful scrutiny to the extreme ratings: the highs and the lows. Therefore managers should take extra care that they have (and that they present) all the data they need to back up those ratings. If there's ever arbitration or any other outside scrutiny of an employee's performance, those ratings will be studied in more detail, so managers certainly want to make sure that they justify them. In recognition of this fact, many organizations' forms *require* a narrative statements for ratings at the top and bottom of the scale. Unfortunately, this encourages the rater error of central tendency because mid point ratings do not require the extra effort of a narrative statement. I recommend narrative statements for *all* the performance objectives and performance factors—with special attention to the very high and very low ratings.

Use Language Consistent with Your Form

Managers should use language in the narrative that's consistent with the form, so that anyone looking at the appraisal can easily relate the rating scale to the narrative and can see how they reinforce each other. Furthermore, by keeping the language of the narrative consistent with rating scale the manager is also keeping the language of all of the narratives, for different employees, consistent with each other.

If, in the language of a form, the mid point of the rating scale is "achieved established standards" the manager should not write in the narrative, "did okay" or "performed about average." If the employee achieved the top of the rating scale on a particular objective, "did exceedingly well," or "did great in my book," or "one of the best I've seen this year" just doesn't make it. Instead the manager should say something like, "On this particular objective I feel that Bill surpassed the established standards regularly." Consistent language supports a manager's arguments and makes the overall rating clearer and more defendable.

Be Careful of Giving Assurances or Making Promises

It can be dangerous to make categorical promises in exchange for performance improvements unless managers are sure they can back them up; courts have ruled that there is an implied contract in such statements. That is, if I tell Janet, "Make 150% of your quota next year and you'll be in line to be supervisor!" and Janet does meet her quota but there are no openings for supervisor, the company and I may be in trouble. Legalities aside, it's never a good idea to create misunderstandings with employees. So managers should be very careful to word statements in a way that is consistent with reality. Managers can suggest the possibility of advancement or reward, if such possibilities exist, but all the "ifs" need to be included. "Were you to achieve this level you'd be eligible for possible advancement *if there were such opportunities.*"

PART III

The Performance Appraisal Discussion

CHAPTER TEN

Preparing for the Discussion and Building a Productive Atmosphere

With this section of the book we have arrived at last at the least popular phase of the performance management process, the part which contains the greatest potential for conflict and misunderstanding, the part that's hardest to predict or control. Now is when managers may have to tell at least some of their employees why they think there are flaws in the employees' performance, and in the face of their reactions to that unpleasant news, get them to cooperate on a plan for the next appraisal period. What if the employee gets red in the face and starts accusing you? What if (as will happen more often) they just nod politely and pretend to cooperate while subtly dragging their feet every second of the discussion?

Even so this is potentially the most productive part of the process. This is where a manager can really begin to put the performance appraisal to work. This is when managers can trouble-shoot productivity problems and get employees to "buy-in" to steps for performance improvement.

As a manager prepares to meet this challenge, he or she should be encouraged to learn that this step in the performance management process is not as fluid or slippery as it may first appear. Any personal interaction is less predictable than the procedures by which a person can manipulate a stack of forms. But if approached properly, the performance appraisal discussion is a carefully structured interaction that a manager can guide and control by using the tools I'm going to introduce in the next several chapters.

PREPARING FOR THE DISCUSSION

Adequate preparation for the performance appraisal discussion can go a long way toward making the process more efficient and effective.

Employee's Self-Evaluation

As I indicated in Chapter Four, where an "ideal" version of the performance appraisal form and process is presented, to make the discussion as effective and productive as possible, the performance appraisal process should include the employee's input. This is a step that is usually omitted. A few weeks prior to the actual appraisal discussion and prior to writing up the appraisal, a manager should ask the employee to do a self-appraisal, and schedule a separate meeting to discuss the employee's perspective.

If work schedules and the organization's policies permit managers to request an employee self-appraisal, with a separate meeting to discuss it, I strongly recommend that they include it—it's proven to be the best way to prepare for the performance appraisal discussion. Two to three weeks prior to the appraisal discussion, the manager should talk with the employee, reminding him or her of the upcoming appraisal. The manager should solicit an employee self-evaluation, remind the employee of the criteria for which they will be evaluated, perhaps give them a copy of the form, or a modified version of it, and schedule a time to meet and discuss the employee's self-appraisal. In Chapter Eleven you'll find a Discussion Guide which will help you to get the most out of this type of meeting, and as you'll see, the nature of the final discussion will be significantly affected by it. The manager should make it clear that the employee is not writing his or her own appraisal, but that input is needed prior to the writing of the final appraisal.

If for any reason a manager does not plan to get employee input, at least a few days prior to the appraisal discussion, the manager should remind the employee of the upcoming appraisal; remind them of the criteria on which the evaluation will be based, and, if possible, work out an exact time for the discussion that's mutually agreeable.

Scheduling the Meeting

By suggesting that the schedule be at a "mutually agreeable" time I don't mean to imply that the manager will leave it up to the employee to decide when the appraisal will take place (for some employees the answer would be never); but negotiating this element can be worthwhile because with the employee's input the manager can schedule an hour when the employee's full attention is guaranteed. It may turn out that while an hour can be carved out between two and three on Thursday, the employee will be so involved with a project at that time that he or she won't really be able to pay full attention; or maybe between now and next Thursday the employee won't have time to prepare properly. If possible, it's better to reschedule a time when both parties are able to concentrate and which affords them sufficient time to prepare.

No Hints

Whatever they do, managers should not inform their employees of their final conclusions or ratings. It may, of course, be obvious based on interactions with the employee all year long: in that event, there's no point in telling employees what they already know. If it isn't obvious, there's nothing to be gained by letting them spend the time between now and the scheduled discussion worrying about it. It would be wrong to say: "Oh Bill, as you know, we have your performance appraisal discussion coming up next week, and by the way, we've got some heavy stuff to discuss." Bill would not enjoy his weekend very much and his suffering would serve no purpose. And on the other hand, it's just as bad to say, "And by the way, Bill, there's nothing to worry about, so relax." That would reduce the incentive to prepare. Instead, Bill should be reminded of the criteria for the appraisal, and asked either to prepare a self-evaluation or at least to think about his performance and any relevant information or questions he'd like to bring up at the discussion.

Assembling Data

Now that the manager has prepared the employee, the manager should get prepared by assembling all the materials and all the required forms, including the employee performance data collected during the appraisal period. The manager should review each rating and verify the evidence for each judgment. Getting the employees to accept the conclusions could be an essential step on the road toward winning their cooperation in any recommended changes. If the manager has the employee's self-appraisal, he or she will know what areas of disagreement to expect and should review them in preparation for the final performance appraisal discussion.

Securing a Meeting Room

A meeting room should be scheduled for the appointed time and arrangements made to avoid interruptions if at all possible: having a lot of people interrupt with calls and questions during the appraisal will reduce both parties' concentration, might be perceived as a discourtesy by the employee, and certainly would work against the atmosphere the manager wants to create for this discussion.

What kind of a room is ideal for conducting a discussion of this kind? Some managers specify a "neutral location, something which doesn't emphasize my authority." In other words, a place other than that manager's office. The fact is, however, that wherever the discussion takes place, the manager is still the employee's boss, and the authority transfers. It's how managers conduct the discussion and their relationship with the employee that's going to make it go smoothly or not.

It is more important to obtain a room which is private. Privacy, ideally, means a room with a door that shuts and walls that go to the ceiling. If a manager's office is a cubical it might be better to borrow a conference room or some other place for this discussion. However, there may not be that option. In that event, you may want to remember what a man-

ager once told me about conducting selection interview: "I have to interview in a cubical. So what I do
is, I stand up on my chair before I bring the candidate in and I say to everybody, 'Will you keep it
down out there? I'm going to be having a private
discussion—go get a cup of coffee or something.'"
While a bit extreme, it might be useful to at least
alert others that a private discussion with an employee is taking place and gain their cooperation. It
might seem like a little thing, but at least it stops
the giggling in the next cubical, and that's important. Those giggles may have nothing to do with
the employee, but the employee doesn't necessarily
know that.

Whether there is laughter or not, if they hear
voices in the next cubical, employees will be un-
pleasantly reminded of the fact that everything *they*
say can be heard. When I was in a doctor's office
not long ago, sitting in the waiting room, I noticed
that I could hear every word exchanged between
the doctor and the patient ahead of me. It wasn't
hard for me to make the deductive leap to the realization that when my turn came everyone else in
the waiting room was going to be entertained by an
account of *my* symptoms. It didn't lend itself to a
lot of candor when I was face to face with the doctor,
and of course he couldn't fathom why I wasn't com-
plying with his requests to "speak up"!

If managers have to conduct a performance appraisal in circumstances that aren't conducive to total privacy, they should at least acknowledge that
they wish it were different. So one would say, "Well,
Fred, I realize that it's a little awkward here, I wish
I could have arranged for more privacy. I'd appreciate your help in making the best of it." That way
manager and employee are in it together and the
spirit of cooperation is maintained.

BUILDING A PRODUCTIVE ATMOSPHERE

Once managers have prepared for the performance appraisal, the next key element to consider is the atmosphere or tone of the discussion. A productive atmosphere is relaxed, comfortable, relatively informal, and characterized by mutual trust and respect.

Managers should avoid a formal, stiff, one-sided fact-giving monologue and achieve, as much as possible, an interaction that is relatively informal though still businesslike. This tone is desirable because it actually increases the productivity of the discussion. It minimizes defensiveness and it builds a working relationship; circumstances under which performance improvement is more likely. It also creates a positive impression of the interaction even in employees for whom the feedback may have been negative. Even if I am not able to pat Frank on the back about every aspect of his performance, I've made it clear that I really am concerned about him.

Above all, an atmosphere like the one I've described is productive because it increases spontaneity as the employee responds to the manager's questions. You may wonder what is so important about spontaneity under these circumstances. If managers are using the interaction to its best advantage, to solve problems as well as deliver judgments, they'll want to get information from the employees. What was really behind that performance problem? Managers can ask specific questions (and later I'll be discussing probing techniques that will help you ask more effective questions) but they could never think of *all* the questions they may need to ask because there are too many possibilities. The underlying issues may include aspects that would never occur to the manager. To get that kind of information, managers have to encourage the employees to volunteer it.

That's why creating a spontaneous atmosphere can make such a difference. Factual answers to factual questions are useful, but if a manager can get the employee to answer a question *and then elaborate on it*, that additional subtlety is almost always useful data. A relatively relaxed atmosphere encourages people to say what's really bothering them and when that happens managers know they're getting somewhere.

In the beginning of any meeting there are a number of simple things managers can do to influence the tone of the ensuing discussion. They're so obvious that one may take them for granted, but they should not be overlooked or omitted. A polite initial greeting, for example, is not just a social amenity, but helps to reduce tension when taken seriously. So at the beginning of the discussion managers should be sure to call employees by name and thank them for coming. Then a few minutes of small talk can be useful to further reduce tension and get them used to talking as well as listening.

Of course, whatever is done at this stage of the discussion should reflect the nature of the manager's relationship with the employee. Suppose that throughout the year I have many meetings with a particular employee and I've always begun with a reference to sports or by asking how the kids are doing . . . I should do that now too. If, on the other hand, I have a more formal relationship with the employee, it may seem odd if I sit down and say, "Well, how are your kids doing?" In reality I might not even know the kids' names or how many there are! Use common sense. The start of the performance appraisal discussion should be an extension of what's been going on all year.

The initial atmosphere of the performance appraisal discussion is going to be different for every employee because each employee brings different expectations to the meeting. A number of different factors influence these expectations. One is their experience of the job itself. After all, if Larry hates his job, hates to come in every day, is only there to collect his paycheck, and would just as soon sleep the rest of the week, then he's not going to come into the performance appraisal really motivated to change or get feedback. Those are the facts about him that must be acknowledged.

Another factor is how the employee has been rated on past performance appraisals. Suppose, for example, that for the past three years previous bosses have rated the same Larry we described above "very good," "very good" and "very good" in his performance reviews—essentially just for showing up each day. Larry isn't going to expect much difference in his appraisal, and when it *is* different, the new boss can expect to encounter consternation, concern, and awkwardness.

The most powerful factor affecting the expectations employees bring to the performance appraisal discussion and the resulting initial atmosphere, is the manager's ongoing relationship with the employee. Has the manager

1. given periodic progress reviews during the year?
2. previously been harsh with the employee?
3. previously been pleasant, but not very attentive to specifics?
4. not given the employee much attention all year?
5. shown concern for the person and for his/her performance?

Hopefully, throughout this performance appraisal period, the manager has done the first and last items on the above list. If he or she has given the employee periodic progress reviews all during the year there won't be many surprises in store in this discussion—that will reduce tension considerably. If the manager has shown concern for the employee as an individual and concern for that person's performance, the employee won't be coming in with a chip on his or her shoulder.

However, if the manager has been harsh during the year, a little abrupt, and undiplomatic ("Do this" as opposed to "Would you mind?"), that's going to affect the frame of mind the employee brings to this discussion. On the one hand, the manager may have given them close supervision all year. On the other hand, they may be surprised to find that you're their boss! Obviously, these factors are going to affect the tone of the discussion as well.

What a manager does all year to make the performance appraisal productive will have more to do with the overall tone of the discussion than anything you can do now. See Chapters Thirteen and Fourteen for techniques and strategies that will help you to maintain rapport and cope with defensiveness during the performance appraisal discussion.

CHAPTER ELEVEN

Structuring the Performance Appraisal Discussion

One of the most common mistakes made by managers is to begin the performance appraisal discussion without a clear plan for accomplishing the goals of the meeting. In this chapter I'm going to give you the outline of a structure I suggest my clients use for the performance appraisal discussion. Clients may not use the exact structure or words I use here, but I can't recommend too strongly that they do employ an orderly logical plan or structure, one that will help them accomplish all the goals they want to accomplish during the discussion and covers all the subjects they want the discussion to cover.

If you are able to follow my suggestion and conduct an employee self-appraisal session prior to the final performance appraisal discussion, you'll have two meetings with the employee: one to discuss their unofficial self-appraisal and one to discuss your official appraisal. I've supplied two discussion guides to help you structure those meetings. If, on the other hand, you *don't* have that initial employee self-appraisal meeting, you'll only have one meeting, and you will have to take a significantly different approach to the discussion; in view of this difference I've supplied a third discussion guide. This will help you to structure the meeting when you haven't had a prior employee self-appraisal meeting.

Over the next several pages I'm going to explain some of the fine points on the discussion guides. I'll discuss the last one (no employee pre-meeting) as a variation of the other two, so whether or not you plan to obtain an employee self appraisal I suggest that you read the entire chapter covering all three discussion guides.

Of course you may question whether you need any of the discussion guides—it may strike you as odd to see the exact words to say set out on the page. Well, there's no need to use these exact words, or to use this particular plan. But you will need to have some explicit structure if you want to influence the direction and flow of the discussion and keep both you and the employee from going off on tangents, or getting stuck on one point. Using an orderly plan that schedules time for both you and the employee to raise issues that you consider important will reduce the chance that either of you will leave the meeting feeling thwarted.

As I explain it, bear in mind that the structure presented here is just an outline of the discussion, a road map, if you will. A fuller understanding of the inner workings of the full discussion will come as you read the ensuing chapters on listening skills, questioning techniques, and handling defensiveness.

We'll start with the "Employee Self-Evaluation Discussion Guide."

EMPLOYEE SELF-EVALUATION DISCUSSION

(Employee Does Prework)

GREETING
(Friendly but brief)   *Probe with:*   *What . . .   Who . . .*
                                            Tell me . . .   How . . .
                                            Review . . .   Why . . .
                                            Explain . . .   When . . .
                                            Give me an example . . .

OPENING

I've been looking forward to this chance to talk with you about your work, and I think this discussion can be helpful for both of us. We'll start by reviewing this past year, and then we'll discuss where we go from here.

A good way to start would be for you to review with me your ratings and comments. When we get together for our performance appraisal meeting, I'll give you my perspective, so we can compare. While I'm responsible for the final ratings, I want to give you the opportunity to tell me your point of view.

The small print in the upper right corner of the Discussion Guide—"Probe with: what . . . Tell me . . . Review . . . Explain . . . Give me an example . . ." may seem a bit cryptic at this point. That's because they are meant to remind the manager of the probing techniques which are introduced in Chapter Thirteen. In all of the discussions—Employee Self-Evaluation, Performance Appraisal Discussion (Employee Does Prework), and Performance Appraisal Discussion (No Employee Prework)—it's important that the manager be able to exercise probing and listening skills to get as much high quality information from the employee as possible, but it's especially important in this meeting because the purpose of it is specifically to get input from the employee. The employee should be doing most of the talking, and the manager should be able to draw them out, to get their point of view, even with those employees who aren't particularly articulate or are for some reason reticent about explaining themselves. Chapter Thirteen presents a number of techniques which will help to accomplish that goal.

Otherwise, the general purpose of most of this first part should be pretty clear. The form reminds managers of the social amenities (GREETING) which can be important in establishing a relaxed atmosphere, and provides them with a suggested opening statement to get the ball rolling.

I don't expect that managers will read this opening statement to the employee; I don't advise them to memorize and recite it. What managers say to begin the discussion is up to them and it will sound more natural if they put it in their own words.

But I do advise that, whatever the manager says to the employee to begin the discussion, the points that I've set forth in this sample be made.

I've been looking forward to this chance to talk with you about your work, and I think this discussion can be helpful for both of us.

Two points are made with this statement which managers may tend to dismiss as soft soap, but they shouldn't be omitted without at least thinking about the purposes they serve.

1. "I've been looking forward to this chance . . ." Well, maybe the manager has been dreading it! But the manager should be looking forward to the discussion in at least one sense: it's a chance to accomplish something. The discussion isn't just

an ordeal that the manager and employee have to get through—as a matter of fact.

2. "This discussion can be helpful to both of us." That's exactly right. The discussion is not going to be simply a matter of handing the employee a report card. It's not about delivering the bad news or the good news. It's about what happened this appraisal period, and how that affects what the manager and the employee will be doing during the next appraisal period. It's not about punishment or reward; it's about problem solving, if problems exist.

The second paragraph attempts to minimize any potential defensiveness and establishes the manager's control over the discussion by telling the employee exactly what to expect, especially making it clear that they will get their chance to respond to the evaluation once it has been explained.

"A good way to start would be for you to review with me your ratings and comments . . ."

This assumes that you are meeting to review the employee's self-evaluation, prior to the performance appraisal meeting. Elsewhere in this book I've explained why I think this is a good idea.

"When we get together for our performance appraisal meeting I'll give my perspective so we can compare."

"My perspective," rather than "then I'll show you where you're wrong," helps establish a tone of reasonableness and sets up some of the discussion that will follow—wherever the manager's evaluation is different from the employee's, the manager is going to need to explain why.

"While I'm responsible for the final rating . . ."

A manager does not want to deceive the employee: the manager is going to listen to the employee's point of view and use it as one source of input to write the appraisal; the manager will also eventually give the employee a chance to respond to his or her appraisal. But the manager's evaluation is the evaluation of record and this should be made clear at the outset.

> *". . . I want to give you the opportunity to tell me your point of view, and to ask questions about my ratings and comments."*

This sentence makes it clear that the employee will get a chance to make any comments and ask any questions that he or she feels is necessary. Letting the employee know that up front makes for a more relaxed, less redundant, less time-consuming, more efficient, more productive discussion.

EMPLOYEE'S SELF-EVALUATION

(Have employee take out their completed Performance Appraisal Form, if they have been asked to use it to prepare for the meeting.)

Since you've taken the time to carefully review and complete your copy of the Performance Appraisal Form, let's discuss it. Let's start at the beginning and go through each item one at a time. Let me know what your rating or comment was, and your thinking behind it.

• Take notes	• Do not debate merits
• Listen actively	• Encourage elaboration

Now let me see if I understand. Your overall assessment of your performance in the last year is _____. The areas in which you felt were particularly effective include _____. Finally, the areas in which you feel you might be able to develop or improve include _____. Have I summarized accurately?

(Allow for additional clarification if necessary.)

Again, the form imposes a rational efficient structure on the discussion. The employee will give his or her point of view, taking "each item one at a time," giving the rating for each item, and justifying that rating. The key point to remember during this part of the discussion is that the manager should adhere to the structure as well. His or her evaluation of a given item, maybe *every* item, may be strongly at variance with the employee's. On the other hand, the two may agree one hundred percent. Either way, whether they agree or disagree, the manager should save his or her point of view for later. The manager should not debate the merits of the employee's position now, but try to get a clear understanding of the employee's point of view, exactly what it is, and why things look that way to the employee. The manager's comments and questions should be aimed at reaching that understanding.

Taking notes is advisable precisely because the manager is going to be responding to each item later in the performance appraisal meeting. What I mean by "listen actively" and the techniques managers can use to "encourage elaboration," will be clearer after you've read Chapter Twelve, "Listening Skills," and Chapter Thirteen, "Questioning and Probing Techniques."

The final paragraph of this section instructs the manager to sum up the employee's self-assessment, so that both parties can check the manager's understanding of what has been said by the employee. As always, the exact words the manager uses aren't important, but it is important to make the key points. The employee's overall assessment should be summed up as accurately as possible. Areas in which they thought they were most effective should be listed; then list the areas in which they thought they could develop or improve. Finally, the employee should be asked if the summary is correct.

Occasionally an employee will want to fine-tune

the summary to change emphasis or add information; the manager should not rush things; this lets the employee know that getting the full story is important.

PERFORMANCE APPRAISAL DISCUSSION WITH EMPLOYEE PREWORK

Now, presumably, a few weeks have passed since the employee self-appraisal meeting, the manager has had time to review the self-appraisal and to know where the employee's version differs from his or her own. One advantage of the previous meeting, as we'll see in a moment, is that it allows the manager to give the appraisal both more diplomatically and more persuasively.

MANAGER'S EVALUATION

In our last meeting we went through your review of yourself, now I'd like to share with you my ratings and comments. I'll start with those areas where we generally agree. Then I'll cover the areas in which our views seem to differ, and give you my reasons for my view.

For areas of agreement:
- Acknowledge the merits of employee's reactions
- Add additional information of your own
- Point out where similar ratings are based upon different reasoning if this exists

For areas of disagreement:
- Begin with your higher ratings
- Proceed towards your lowest rating
- Respond to employee's earlier stated points
- Give specific examples
- State your reasons
- Take extra time and care with sensitive areas

End with reference to your overall rating

The greeting should be substantially the same as it was in the previous meeting and serves the same function. Again you're reminded of the probing tools I'll be showing you in Chapter Thirteen—even though this isn't specifically an employee input meeting, the manager will still want obtain the employee's reactions to the presentation.

The introductory statement, as in the other meeting, structures the meeting in advance by telling what's going to happen.

What was learned from the earlier meeting permits the manager to start with areas of agreement. Some managers might be tempted to do exactly the reverse—save the good news for last and end on an "up" note. In reality, however, beginning with areas of agreement first reduces tension by showing the employee, right away, that there is some common ground and (probably) that all the news is not going to be bad. It's easier to persuade someone when he or she knows that you agree on some things. Furthermore, by going over areas of agreement and telling the employee *why* they agree (which may be different from their reasoning) a manager can use these areas of agreement to model his or her methods for the employee: as a result, the employee will be more easily persuaded when the areas of disagreement are discussed. Employees will be less likely to challenge the fairness or validity of a manager's methods when they've seen the methods work to their benefit.

Presenting areas of agreement first gives the manager an opportunity to show the employee how judgments were made. This is important because ultimately, to the extent possible, the manager wants to convince the employee of the validity of the evaluation. Because the manager is talking about conclusions that the employee doesn't dispute, he or she won't be on the defensive and will therefore find it easy to pay attention to the reasoning. The faith the managers builds in the methods at this point will contribute to the credibility of the presentation a little later, when the manager moves on to the areas of disagreement. That's why, rather than merely saying, "Well, here we're in agreement, let's move on," it's better to give the whole case for each rating. When people agree with us we're not as prone to examine the logic behind their thinking as we are when they disagree. But if we agree for different reasons it's important to make that fact clear—because we both must understand how we reached our conclusions.

All the other suggestions given in the box under "For areas of disagreement" speak to the same purpose of making a convincing case and winning agreement to your point of view. It might take too long to give every incident that contributed to a given conclusion, but the manager should give enough specific examples for clarity and to show evidence for the conclusions. Besides stating his or her reasons, it's very important for the manager to respond to the reasoning the employee gave for his or her different self-assessments with regard to that same issue. If the manager disagrees, obviously the employee's reasoning wasn't convincing; but it's not enough to let that be obvious. In order to convince the employee, the manager must respond to the arguments and explain why he or she disagrees. And finally, common sense dictates taking extra time and care with sensitive issues. With your final rating the "report card" part of the performance appraisal comes to an end.

All these points will help a manager be persuasive and will focus the discussion on the nature of the desired performance—hopefully, not only will the employee be persuaded that the ratings are fair, he or she will come away with a better idea of what is the expected level of performance.

SETTING DEVELOPMENTAL OBJECTIVES

(If strongly held major differences are present, or much time has passed, schedule another meeting to handle the next section, and go to the close.)

Based on what we discussed up to this point, there are several things we can focus on. Some relate to improving your effectiveness in your current role, and others represent areas you may want to develop, or opportunities you want to consider. Let's come up with a list of three to five goals or objectives for the next year and plan ways in which we can make them happen.

- Make written list
- Include aspects of job performance that need improvement
- Include steps for development or advancement
- Identify methods of meeting objectives such as: training, coaching, special projects

---

If at this point manager and employee still have strongly held differences, or if they've spent more time than expected on this phase of the discussion, the manager may decide to postpone the discussion of the next steps to the next meeting. In some organizations, the review of last year is routinely separated from the discussion of plans for the next appraisal period.

Whether at this meeting or in a subsequent meeting, the manager's opening statement is in effect, "the next step is to take what we've learned and build to the future." Then deal with the development plan.

As discussed in Chapter Seven, "Creating an Employee Development Plan," there are two aspects to the development plan. On the one hand, the development plan can be used to increase the employee's effectiveness in their current job. If an employee fell short of the standard in one of the performance objectives or performance factors for the previous appraisal period, if there are skills in which he or she is not fully competent, or areas for improvement, or if the manager has noted underlying causes behind the employee's failure to meet some of the objectives for the past period, the first step in the development plan should be creating developmental objectives which will help the employee improve.

The second aspect of the development plan concerns what the manager can do to help the employee grow; whether that means simply enriching the employee's current job to maintain the current level of interest and motivation or create developmental objectives which will equip them for promotions in the future.

SETTING PERFORMANCE OBJECTIVES

The performance plan is the set of new objectives for that employee for organization during the next year. While you've thought the performance objectives through (see Chapter Five, "Setting Good Performance Objectives), it is important to refine them with the employee. There should be room to involve them in generating the final version of these objectives, especially when it comes to deciding how those objectives are to be achieved. As discussed in Chapter Five, an approach which wins the employee's enthusiastic commitment (perhaps because the employee thought of it) may work better in the long run than an approach which is more efficient in the abstract, but wins only lukewarm cooperation from the employee.

The manager presents the list of performance objectives to the employee one by one, discusses them with the employee, and makes adjustments in the phraseology. If he or she wants to stop short of changing the objectives itself, the manager may make sidebar notes on which both parties agree, clarifying the requirements and the standard for meeting that objective.

CLOSE

In summary, here are the things I'm going to do based upon our discussion, and my understanding of what actions you're going to take. (Read list to employee.) Have I accurately stated what we agreed on?

By the way, how confident are you that you can meet the goals we've set today?

Let's pick a follow-up date to see how we're doing on these issues. (Enter on your calendar.)

As a final matter, it's company policy that we both sign this Performance Appraisal to document that we had this discussion. Please sign and date the form here. (Point to place on form for signature.)

(Offer opportunity for employee to attach a statement if company policy permits.)

Thanks for your cooperation, and I look forward to our next meeting.

Some of the things this part of the form instructs managers to do may seem obvious, and some may seem unimportant. I advise managers, nevertheless, to cover all of them. Even if it's perfectly obvious that an employee understands and agrees to what has just been discussed, it's important to get employee to say so. It is important because, in a certain percentage of cases, managers may be very surprised by what they learn. When, as an offhand statement (because I'm wrapping things up, I'm squaring up papers) I say, "Lawrence, I'm kind of curious, how confident are you that you can actually get these things done next year?" One time out of ten, the employee will take a deep breath and acknowledge, "I don't think I can do it."

In that case I'll be glad I thought to ask the question. Now, I can make some readjustments, renegotiate my agreement with the employee, or find out what the obstacles are and start dealing with them. That is, now, rather than three months from now when I find out things aren't getting done because the employee never really thought he or she could do them to begin with, had strong doubts, and had just gone along with what I said.

Having asked this question and dealt with the answer, the manager develops some follow-up dates, because this is part of an ongoing process, and as a final matter, say: "We need to sign the form as an indication that we've had this discussion. Please sign here."

What if somebody refuses to sign the form? This may be a sign that disagreements still persist between the manager and the employee. Certainly not all such disagreements can be resolved, and the manager is not going to put a gun to the employee's head to get that form signed. You make a note of the fact that you reviewed the appraisal with the employee on this date, that you gave the employee the opportunity to sign it and he or she declined. Some organization's performance appraisal forms include a space where employees can comment on their appraisal: this can be useful as a way employees can register their disagreement while still cooperating with the process as a whole. In other organizations it is policy in cases of disagreement to allow employees to write a separate statement, which is then attached to the performance appraisal form. I think that there is much to be said for giving employees the opportunity to comment for the record when they feel strongly about an issue; on the other hand, I would not want them to feel obligated to make a statement. If it is to be a section of the form, its use should be clearly optional.

PERFORMANCE APPRAISAL DISCUSSION WITH NO EMPLOYEE PREWORK

The meeting opens with the same greeting. The Discussion Guide again reminds the manager of the probing tools; the difference between the two versions begin after the opening statement.

PERFORMANCE APPRAISAL
DISCUSSION GUIDE
(No Employee Prework)

GREETING
(Friendly but brief)   *Probe with*   *What . . .*   *Who . . .*
                                              Tell me . . .   *How . . .*
                                              Review . . .   *Why . . .*
                                              Explain . . .   *When . . .*
OPENING   *Give me an example . . .*

I've been looking forward to this chance to talk with you about your work, and I think this discussion can be helpful for both of us. We'll start by reviewing this past year, and then we'll discuss where we go from here.

PRESENTING THE APPRAISAL

A good way to start would be for me to walk you through my appraisal. While I'm responsible for the final ratings, I want to give you the opportunity to ask questions and give me your point of view. We'll go over the entire form, then we'll talk it over.

One way of describing the difference between the "Employee does Pre-work" and the "No Employee Pre-work" versions of the Discussion Guide is that instead of opening the discussion with the manager's response to *the employee's* self-appraisal, the manager gives his or her views and ratings first, and then gives *the employee* a chance to respond to it. Because the manager doesn't know in advance what the areas of disagreement are or what are the particularly sensitive issues, he or she would begin with a *quick scan* of Parts I, II and III (if following my form): this is the "report card" part of the form. The manager presents the ratings for performance objectives and performance factors, and the overall rating. Don't hand over the form to the employee. Place it on the desk so they can see it and go over the form with them.

EMPLOYEE'S REACTIONS

Now that we have gone over the form, let's discuss it. Take your time and give me your overall reaction, then give me your reactions to specific items.

• Take notes	• Do not debate merits
• Listen actively	• Encourage elaboration

Now let me see if I understand. Your overall reaction to my evaluation is _____. More specifically, you tend

to agree with my ratings in the following areas _____.
On the other hand you have a different view of _____.
Have I summarized accurately?

(Allow for additional clarification if necessary.)

In a way, as the manager, I will try now to accomplish the goals of the employee self-appraisal meeting. I want to learn the employee's point of view so I can respond and make my case more persuasively. Remember the more convincing I can be, the more employee buy-in I can get for the future.

To respond to the employee's point of view, I have to make certain that I indeed have it, so I run it by him or her to make sure. This also let's the employee know that I've heard and understood his or her remarks.

MANAGER'S RESPONSE AND DISCUSSION

Now let's take those items where we seem to differ. We'll cover them one at a time, and I want you to see how I came to my conclusions. I would like to come to a common understanding on each issue if we can, but if not, at least I want to be sure that we both clearly see the basis for each other's point of view.

• Review one at a time	• Use active listening
• Give specific examples	• Take extra time and care with sensitive areas

End with reference to overall rating

We start with areas of disagreement, because the employee has already seen my ratings and is focused on where we disagree: it won't be possible to postpone discussion of those issues. It isn't ideal to start with these issues, but that's one of the prices of not obtaining employee input in advance.

The purpose here is essentially the same as in the "disagreement" section of Version 1. Disagreement may still exist when this part of the discussion is over, but at least it will be clear that my ratings are not arbitrary, and the understanding of my reasoning and methods can provide a basis for the development plan to come. The remainder of the discussion is identical in both versions. You move on to the development plan, the performance plan, and the close.

CHAPTER TWELVE

Listening Skills

In the performance appraisal discussion, in addition to presenting information, a manager is going to try to get information from the employee about what's happening in the work place—and about what reactions that employee is having. The listening skills and probing techniques described in the following pages are designed to help you do that more effectively.

In this chapter and the next one I'll be talking about some things that we take for granted—the value of comments, where to insert a pause, when and when not to ask questions that can be answered simply "yes" or "no." It may not be apparent why I am presenting as special techniques things you already do in everyday conversation. The difference, however, is that in ordinary conversation you use these techniques automatically and unconsciously: my aim is to show you how to deploy them purposefully in the pursuit of specific goals, and to use them in a context in which it is all to easy to forget about them entirely.

COMMENTS

For example, often, in their eagerness to get to the bottom of things, managers will shoot a battery of questions at their employees. Each reply is followed immediately by another question.

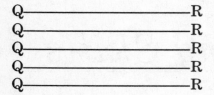

This is a diagram of an interrogation, not a smooth conversational flow. By the time the manager reaches the fifth question–response without supplying any feedback—without giving the employee any indication of how the answers were received—the employee is reduced to saying, "Yes." "That's correct." "There were three." "I understand."

There are at least three reasons why it's better to comment between questions, and why it's worth while to make an active attempt to master the use of comments as a skill and apply it to the performance appraisal.

COMMENTS CREATE A SMOOTH
CONVERSATIONAL FLOW

The first reason, as I've hinted above, is that commenting is necessary for maintaining rapport during the discussion. Commenting sustains the semblance of a relaxed conversational flow even when the focus is on drawing data out of the employee. The manager simply inserts a comment in between the employee's reply and his or her next question. "What were some of the obstacles in getting that project to completion on time?" The employee responds. The manager then says, "Oh, I didn't realize it was that complex. I can see some unexpected events came up that made it difficult. What did you do when that happened?" The insertion of the comment—a reaction, a summarization—shows the manager is thinking about it and taking it into account, and as a result the whole tone of the interaction changes. It sounds more like a conversation.

After all, this is the way people speak. In ordinary conversation people do not just fire questions at one another. Suppose you meet a friend whom you haven't seen in a while, how does the conversation go?

Q: "I haven't seen you in a while, where have you been?"
A: "I've been on vacation."
Q: Where did you go?"
Q: "How long were you away?"
Q: "Why did you choose a cruise?"
Q: "How big was the ship?"
Q: "What ports did you stop at?"

Does that sound like an ordinary conversation? It sounds like a scene from "Dragnet," right? This is the sort of conversation Sergeant Friday had all the time. If, in ordinary conversation, you talk to people like this, people say things like, "Are you writing a book? You work for the FBI?" It sounds intrusive.

In real life, comments or reactions would bridge an answer to the next question, making the exchange more conversational. It would probably go more like this:

Q: "I haven't seen you a while, where have you been?"

A: "I've been on vacation."

C–Q: "Really? Usually I go away in the middle of the summer, but it's not a bad idea to take it now. Where'd you go?"

A: "I went on a cruise."

C–Q: "A cruise? I don't think I could do that. I think I'd get cabin fever if I had to stay in one place that long. Of course it would depend on the size of the ship. How big was your ship?"

And so on. When we speak we do not use Aristotelian logic, moving from premise to conclusion. A conversation is organic. We ask a question, they respond, we react to it, and then we ask something else. Conversations which proceed in this fashion are what we're used to, and they make for a lot less tension than the interrogational style.

COMMENT ELICITS MORE SPONTANEOUS INFORMATION

The second advantage of bothering to engage in this process concerns an issue I've raised earlier: spontaneity. The manager asks the employee a question, gets a response, and comments on it, exactly the way you did before, but last time you used it only as a bridge to the next question. This time you *pause* for a second as you seem to be considering what they've said.

You've asked them a question, they've answered. Now you comment on it, and pause. You say, "I didn't realize it was that complex, Bob, it does seem like there was a lot more going on than I'd imagined, including the fact that you had to wait a long time for those reports." And pause three seconds. Often the employee will volunteer additional data spontaneously, without your having to ask a question. This spontaneous data is only available as a result of commenting with a pause. The manager couldn't have thought of the question to ask to get this information. It's not an intellectual answer. It's just a continuing flow of data, and is not likely to be understood in any other way. In many circumstances it's highly significant—what they say at this point may be the *real* problem and the *real* objection.

So that's the second advantage of commenting. You actually get more data. Commenting encourages employees to volunteer subtleties about which you might never think to inquire.

COMMENTING GIVES YOU A TACTFUL WAY TO INTERRUPT

On the other hand, sometimes employees volunteer too much data. A manager may ask employees a question, they answer and—forget it, they're not stopping. If the manager doesn't find some way to stop them, the employees will go on for another twenty minutes giving more data, more clarification, more justification, either because they're nervous or because it's just their style. Managers are responsible for the breadth, depth, scope of the discussion, therefore, they must have some way of controlling or guiding it.

Commenting can be an invaluable technique at this point. The manager can actually gently interrupt the employee's response with a comment, change the subject, or back up to something that was skipped over. The conscious use of comments enables the manager to direct the conversation tactfully, without damaging rapport. As the employee proceeds down a particular path the manager can make an intervention, thus re-directing the subject down a different path. "Well, Keith, I didn't realize it was that complex." (The manager acknowledges what has been said.) "But—who did you speak to over there?" The manager redirects him. This is quite different from saying, "Whoa, wait a minute! Hold it! I don't want to talk any more about this. I'm changing the subject. Let's go on to something else." In fact, the employee may hardly know what the manager has done. It's just that the conversation is now about something else.

The manager simply reacts to what is being said and changes course.

There are other advantages to commenting. Arguably it makes the manager into a better, more attentive listener—one can't summarize what has been said unless he or she has been paying attention and absorbing what is being said. Finally it gives the manager time to think.

The employee can't go anywhere while the manager is commenting.

These other advantages are worth remembering, but the first three items—making it conversational, getting spontaneous information, allowing you to guide and direct the discussion—are the main reasons why mastering comments as a conscious active skill can make an enormous difference in the performance appraisal discussion.

TYPES OF COMMENTS

Managers won't find grunts and exclamations on the list of comments presented here. An occasional "Mmnnn," "aha," "aw," "Hmmmm" could help, but by themselves these sounds don't give the employee

the sense that the manager is really paying attention. They're not going to get the manager the advantages we've talked about. In fact the whole world
of so-called "casuals" (including "great," "swell,"
"fine," "good," and "that's interesting") are rather
ineffectual for these purposes.

If the employee says, "Well, this part of my job
really is, well, like a black hole. I'm putting a lot of
effort in. But nothing really happens, I never see
any results" and I say, "Well, that's interesting,"
the employee may get the impression I'm not taking
him or her seriously or didn't appreciate the signif-
icance of what was being said.

One of our goals is to let employees know that
we're listening and paying attention. The comments
I'm about to discuss accomplish that because they
indicate an awareness of the substance of the employee's statement.

Restatement

Summarize the employee's statement back to them.
If I pause afterward, it might get the employee to
elaborate further. Instead of asking a question, make
a comment such as "It sounds like you worked on
several ways to solve that problem" and pause, at
which point the employee may spontaneously add to
a previous statement some clarification or explanation. Restatement can also ensure that I have indeed
gotten the employee's message correctly. If I misunderstood, my restatement gives the employee the
opportunity to set the record straight. Used without
a pause it can accomplish our other advantages of
making the discussion seem conversational, or I can
use it to exercise control over the flow of information.

Pat on the Back

Recognizing an employee's achievements by positively commenting on them is a powerful technique for eliciting more information and maintaining good will. By positively reinforcing the employee for achievements, I have an opportunity to gain the employee's confidence and indicate that I understand what I heard and am paying attention. However, I should avoid giving an employee false praise or insincere comments because it can undercut my credibility. I should take the time to react to and comment on genuine positive behavior.

Refocus from Negative to Positive

I want to create an atmosphere in which the employee feels comfortable about sharing potentially negative information. I must not let the employee think I am overvaluing any negative information given to me. When a mistake comes up, I should shift attention to what can be done to correct it. For instance if an employee explains that he or she did not complete a particular aspect of a project, I might say, "That must have been disappointing for you. What can we do to keep that from happening again?" or "You know better than anyone else what was going on there; I'd like to get your side of the story. What do you think were the reasons . . ." It doesn't mean I'm not concerned or determined to get to the bottom of the problem, but I am gaining the employee's cooperation and avoiding unnecessary tension and constriction.

Reflect Feelings

When employees clearly have strong feelings about a particular subject it is often quite effective for the manager to show genuine empathy. Following this with a pause may elicit even more detailed information.

The first of these kinds of comments—restatement—is by a wide margin the most important and the one a manager should use the most frequently. The last three can come in handy: use them if the opportunity arises. If an employee mentions an accomplishment that merits a pat on the back, I'd show I am aware of it: "Well, it sounds to me like you put a lot of extra effort in beyond what you really had to do and I can see it paid off—I think it says something about you, Tom, that you put in that extra effort." If I can say that, well and good; but of course for me to use this technique, it is necessary that the employee first mention a worthy accomplishment.

If employees acknowledge that they didn't do something quite so well—if they say something of a negative nature—then I might downplay it so they realize I'm not overreacting to it. "Jamie, I can see how that was awkward for you, I appreciate your acknowledging the fact the end result was off target. However you were in the middle of it, you know better than anyone else what was going on, I'd like your perspective to understand what happened."

If I wanted to move the discussion on: "I can see how there was some awkwardness, but there were lots of areas where you were obviously more effective; let's focus on those issues." So I can downplay it and move on to another issue. I can either explore that issue or pass by it. In either case, it's not that the issue isn't important, but I'm not making a big deal of it.

If the employee obviously has strong feelings about what is being said, I can say, "Well I can see, based on your presumption of what was expected of you, you are a little disappointed then at how this actually worked out." Not that I'm agreeing, but given the employee's understanding and information, I can empathize. That helps maintain rapport.

Restatement is the technique that counts the most because it can be used at any time. Suppose I've asked Ellen four or five questions in a row. The interaction is getting a little tense, and I'd like to make the flow more conversational, but her answer doesn't lend itself to the last three types of comments. I can always summarize back to her what she said.

If this technique is to seem natural and conversational, a manager must not repeat the employee's statement word for word, but be as accurate as possible without adding or subtracting anything and without sharing an assessment of what was said. The manager should just give a reasonably accurate summary.

Summaries and restatements must be complete. Suppose I summarize something that George said and in doing so I leave something out? He thinks I didn't get it. Perhaps he gave me three points. I heard it all, but I only gave him two back. He might say, "Well, Bill, I guess I did say that, but I also meant to suggest . . ." and he repeats the data he thinks I ignored or missed. Instead of getting new or spontaneous data I'm getting a repeat, which is a waste of his time and mine. If I do it a lot he thinks I'm not listening to him.

Suppose I add to what he said. He'll correct me. "I guess I did say that, but I didn't mean to suggest . . ." It's worse if I give the impression that I'm evaluating him, especially during the performance appraisal. "If I understand you correctly, George, it sounds as if you weren't particularly effectual in that area . . ." True, perhaps, but you're not going to get a lot of mileage out of a comment like that.

There are a few tricks I might want to practice which will help me achieve this kind of accuracy and completeness without seeming like a parrot. For one thing, try changing the order of the phrases. If the employee says ABC, I can say CBA or some other version of it. That is, Bob says, "Well, sometimes I get impatient, when people don't quickly pick up when I give instructions and direction." I can say, "I get the impression, Bob, from what you're saying that when you give instruction and direction and people don't pick up quickly, on occasion you get a bit impatient."

All you've done is change the order of the phrases. It will seem like hardly a difference but to the listener it seems like I've massaged what was said. This may never happen to you, but in fact I once made a restatement to someone repeating virtually word for word what he said, merely changing the order of the phrases, and he actually said, "Well, you know Bill, I guess that's what I meant."

On the average managers would probably comment once after every four or five questions, if their goal is to make the process flow conversationally. If a manager is face to face with an employee who is quiet and shy or nervous, he or she might make more comments along with pauses, to encourage that person to volunteer additional data. Asking more questions helps too, but the point is to get more spontaneous data out of the employee.

For the employee who's running on and on, a manager might make a comment every two questions or maybe every question. Not pausing after any of the questions will keep the conversation moving.

You'll find that comments are a handy tool to use in many business situations, whenever it's your responsibility to guide and direct the flow of conversation.

CHAPTER THIRTEEN

Questioning and Probing Techniques

The manager's ability to properly phrase questions to control information flow and elicit more in-depth feedback is a key element of successful performance appraisal discussions. Effective questioning techniques will help the manager get the employee to talk more, determine the accuracy of the employee's perceptions, probe more deeply into those areas where more information is needed and less deeply into others, use time efficiently, and get sufficient information for setting goals and accomplishing them.

In this chapter I'm going to explore some of those questioning techniques. I'll be discussing what sorts of questions to avoid as well as what kinds are especially useful and how to combine the use of different types of questions and comments for maximum effectiveness.

CLOSED-END VS.
OPEN-ENDED QUESTIONS

Sometimes managers inexperienced at conducting fact-probing discussions will find that during the performance appraisal employees are rather unresponsive for no obvious reason. If the manager is having problems such as this, it's possible that without realizing it he or she is doing something to encourage this behavior: perhaps asking a lot of closed-end questions.

A closed-end question is simply a question which could be answered by the single word yes or no. In everyday life we use them all the time. "Is the meeting still scheduled?" "Are there any alternatives to that approach?" "If we could resolve that problem, would you be able to sign the contract?" "Are my shirts back from the cleaners?"

There's nothing inherently wrong with closed-end questions: they're efficient and effective if used in the right context. However, in the performance appraisal (or whenever you want to get a lot of full rich data from another person) it's advisable to have conscious control of this question form. In fact you should, as a rule, avoid them in the performance appraisal.

There are three reasons managers should avoid closed-end questions. In the first place, some individuals, because they are nervous, shy or literal minded, will answer closed-end questions with a single yes or no. For the most part a lot of "yeses" and "nos" aren't going to help me very much when I want to find out what went wrong on the job and how it can be prevented in the future.

Secondly, even with employees who are more forthcoming, closed-end questions tend to restrict the range of the response. When employees hear a lot of closed-end questions ("Is there . . ." "Are you . . ." "Can there . . ." "Should there . . ." "Were there . . ." "Could you") the message they get is: "Stick to the point, don't elaborate, just give me the facts." A chain of closed-end questions subliminally communicates a request to be brief. After such an experience individuals say, "Well, I would have liked to elaborate, but he wanted me to be brief, and I didn't want to offend him."

And the third reason managers should avoid closed-end questions is that verbally skilled employees who find a given topic awkward can use a closed-end question to change the subject. Managers can easily lose control of the discussion that way. This is a technique used by politicians who are asked a question, which they answer briefly with great directness: The reporter says: "Don't you feel that—" and the politician answers: "Absolutely. And furthermore—" and from then on, naturally, they're talking about something completely different. Some employees may know that technique, too.

There are times when a closed-end question comes in handy in the performance appraisal. I may find it useful to ask, "Isn't it true, Jean, that those reports, three times out of five, came in more than a week late?" Here my use of the closed-end question is similar to the salesperson's use: "If we could resolve that would you be able to sign the contract?" They want agreement and commitment. I want Jean to at least acknowledge that there is a problem, so I can focus on solutions. I use a closed-end question to get that reluctant acknowledgment, and Jean says, "Well, y-y-y-ess."

Nevertheless, when I'm trying to gather information, closed-end questions should be the exception, not the rule. Usually it's preferable to ask open-ended questions. Open-ended questions encourage employees to elaborate, gives them the sense that the manager is interested in hearing more, and actually draw them out more. Open-ended questions begin with: "What . . ." "How . . ." "Why . . ." "Tell me . . ." "Who . . ." "Explain . . ." "Give me an example . . ." "Describe . . ."

"What are some of the reasons you approached the problem that particular way?"
"How'd you go about resolving it?"
"Why did you use that approach?"
"Tell me who you spoke to over there."
"Explain to me your rationale for that action."
"Give me an example of the intervention you made to deal with that problem as it came up."
"Describe to me step-by-step the way you proceeded."

Open-ended questions, in turn, fall into a couple of further categories. There are five types of open-ended questions, each of which serve unique purposes and give the manager greater control over the depth and subtlety of the information obtained.

ONE-STEP PROBES

I call "One-Step Probes" open-ended questions that introduce new areas or begin new topics. The most common one-step probes are questions that begin with the word "What." They may also begin with words or phrases such as "Describe," "Explain," "Tell me." Examples of one-step probes are:

"What were some of your major accomplishments during this review period?"

"Tell me about the steps you took to solve that problem."

"Describe the primary obstacles to reducing our level of noncomformance."

"Explain the key factors that led to your success in achieving that objective."

TWO-STEP PROBES

One-step probes open doors for further inquiry. The answers to one-step probes may not give managers all the information they need, or may require clarification. Two-step probes delve deeper into the subject. They typically begin with the words "How, Why, Who, When or Which." A two-step probe also allows managers to test the validity and accuracy of the information employees have shared, while at the same time getting richer and more detailed information. It helps to explore an area opened up by a one-step probe and enables you to properly gauge the accuracy of the initial response. If employees are covering up or exaggerating, they will have difficulty continuing an extensive discussion. In this way a two-step probe—(or a "three-step-", "four-step-" or "five-step probe, for nothing prevents you from delving as far into a given topic as you want) helps the manager uncover accurate information, because employees tend to reply truthfully to direct detailed questions.

The whole process might work like this. I begin by asking, "John, what were some of the obstacles you faced in getting that project done on time?" That's my one-step probe.

"Well," says John, "the data I need to do my end of it comes from another department and I simply can't get the information from them on time. No matter what I do it doesn't come. That's why I was behind on my reports three out of five times. It really wasn't my responsibility, because I was ready to go. As a matter of fact, once I got the data I had it turned around by the next day."

Many a manager would accept this explanation at face value and move on to another subject. It's the easiest thing to do; or perhaps they would take the responsibility to intervene with that other department. Yet there might be much more involved here. Perhaps John himself isn't aware of the real obstacles.

A two-step probe takes matters at least a step further: "Who did you actually speak to in order to get the information on time?" Maybe John's talking to the wrong person.

Or: "When did you speak to them?"

Maybe he requested it too late, or approached that department at an awkward time in the activity cycle.

Or: "How did you go about requesting the data?"

Maybe the way he went about it indicates a lack of awareness of the political dynamics over there.

Or: "Which forms did you ask them to complete?"

Maybe he's sending the wrong form. If it takes them twice as long to complete it, no wonder it's late getting back to him.

This level of detail is necessary to really understand what is behind the problem. Managers should be careful when they're conducting this sort of discussion not to seem unnecessarily aggressive or challenging. "Why" questions can seem threatening if managers don't use just the right tone. Simply to fire the question "Why'd you do it that way?" can seem harsh. They should put it this way: "Given the options, why did you choose that approach instead of one of the others?" The manager is not saying the employee's decision was necessarily wrong; the manager just wants his or her reasoning. Make that clear.

In practice two step probing can be softened in tone by combining them with the listening skills presented in the previous chapter. "What were some of the obstacles you faced in getting the reports in on time," I ask. John answers. And then I comment on what he said before I go on. "Well, John, I get the impression that the information you needed to do your reports reached you a day or two late on a regular basis, which resulted in *your* report being late." I pause for three seconds, and maybe he'll add further clarification without my having to ask. If not, I go on to the two-step probe. I've asked the question I need to ask, but I've preserved a less agressive, more conversational tone.

OTHER QUESTIONING TECHNIQUES

Some employees will be very articulate analytical thinkers who will readily grasp what the manager's driving at and give the needed information. Inevitably, others will not. There are all kinds of employees, and the stress of the performance appraisal discussion will not make it easier for those who have trouble expressing themselves. The questions that follow are designed to help break a log jam when the conversation isn't going anywhere, particularly when the employee blocks on a two-step probe. Because how or why they acted is often of critical importance, their momentary inability to respond is something managers should be able to resolve.

Multiple Choice Questions

Suppose an employee becomes blocked after a two-step probe and cannot readily answer a "how" or "why" question. Not everyone is introspective and some employees have been on automatic and need prompting to give detailed explanations. In such cases you might prompt the employee by giving a list of possible answers, or multiple choices. Provide three or four alternative answers. The employee might choose one of them and expand on it, or the process might spark an idea or jog the employee's memory and the employee will come up with another answer. By giving a series of options, but leaving it open ended, the manager avoids leading the employee to give an expected or "right" answer. At the same time, he or she is helping the employee to overcome a mental block. In using the multiple choice technique, the manager should provide a list of options in the question.

"Over the past six months, you obviously have done better. What are some of the things you might have done that would account for your success? Perhaps you paid more attention to detail; followed the revised instructions; checked with co-workers more frequently; or something else?" This question form tends to get employees to think out loud.

Plural vs. Singular

Questions that are phrased in the singular, such as "What is the one thing that you had the most trouble with on that job" or "What was your most important accomplishment?" are rather direct and can seem too aggressive. The tone does not facilitate a smooth conversational flow. It's better to phrase questions in the plural: "What were some of the things that you had trouble with on that job," or "What were some of your accomplishments?" Otherwise, the manager is putting the employee on the spot, having to decide "the" most important accomplishment. It comes across like a test question. In talking to others in performance appraisals, coaching sessions or in our personal life, the plural form is softer, seems more neutral, and is less likely to interrupt the flow of information.

Comparison and Contrast

Questions which focus the conversation on similarities and differences of experiences, rather than on the mere factual recounting of events, are used to help employees organize their responses. They require the employee to answer more thoughtfully. An example of this type of question might be, "In what ways did you handle your successful accounts that differed from your dealing with your less than successful accounts?" This question will probably elicit more and better information than just asking, "How did you handle your successful accounts?"

As in the above example, comparison and contrast questions are especially effective when the manager is trying to focus on a problem area. Managers should ask employees to compare an area in which they performed well with an area in which they were less successful. It again softens the inquiry: using the comparison form allows managers to acknowledge a positive while asking employees to explain why they were less successful in another area.

CHAPTER FOURTEEN

How to Cope with Defensiveness and Facilitate Problem Solving

In this chapter I'm going to return to the question I raised at the onset of this section of the performance appraisal discussion. What if, because of the high stakes and the emotions involved when an employee's work is evaluated, I encounter resistance, anger, or defensiveness during this discussion? It is vitally important to win my employees' agreement about possible problems and commitment to solutions; that's unlikely to occur when they are defensive. Problem solving cannot occur when people are "on-guard." Remember, the anticipation of defensiveness is the number one reason managers give for avoiding or dreading the performance appraisal discussion.

The pages that follow present a model of the emotional dynamic between manager and employee during the performance appraisal discussion, and in the context of that model, I'll show you how to recognize resistance and defensiveness (which are not always obvious) and how to defuse them.

THE FLIGHT/FIGHT CONTINUUM

As you may remember from Psychology 101, there are only two categories of response available to human beings when they're under pressure or stress. Whether there's a truck coming at us at sixty miles per hour or whether we're in the jungle facing a charging lion—or even if the threat is more subtle, such as loss of self esteem, criticism, the perception of being treated unfairly, or any psychological stress— we have two basic choices: we can either stand our ground or fight or get the heck out of there. Fight or flight. In every day life we're all used to seeing the following symptoms of defensiveness, and they all fall into one category or the other:

Fight Response	Flight Response
−Raise voice	−Look away
−Point finger	−Turn away
−Blame others	−Speak softly
−Stare	−Change subject
−Pound desk	−Agree quickly

These two response categories apply during the performance appraisal discussion, both to the employee and to the manager. Of course it's very unlikely managers start by raising their voices or that either employee or manager is going to get up and leave the room. But during the meeting all the other reactions do occur fairly often—one or both parties raising his or her voice, nervous figiting, evasive responses, saying "yes" quickly when there really isn't agreement, or stubbornly sticking to a point that's clearly been refuted—all of those responses fall into one or the other of these categories.

Fight and flight response can be looked on as the opposite extremes of a continuum. Everyone's behavior falls somewhere between these extremes. Most people lean in one direction or the other from the mid-point, depending on their response style, personality, or their perception of how to handle a particular situation. Normal responses range between assertive behavior and open/receptive behavior. It is when behavior reaches past these points that defensiveness and lowered ability to engage in problem solving occurs.

Let the vertical line in Figure 14.1 represent me, the manager. Obviously, I don't want to start out in the extreme fight or flight mode. My behavior will probably fall—and should fall—somewhere near the middle of the chart. If I'm like most people it probably won't be in the exact midpoint; it will be a little above or below it. Assuming that my natural style is nearer "fight" than "flight," what would be a productive level of this quality? What would we call it? "Assertive," perhaps. "Let me tell you what I think

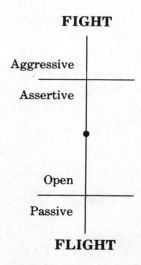

FIGURE 14.1 The Manager.

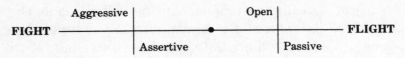

FIGURE 14.2 The Employee.

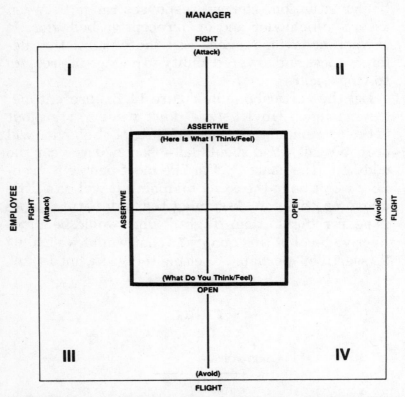

FIGURE 14.3 Conflict Interaction Analysis. (© 1991 Swan Consultants, Inc.)

about that issue," is a typical statement in this mode. If I were to behave aggressively, I'd be over the line.

Suppose my natural style is to lean in the direction of the flight mode. The word for this style might be "open." "What do you think about this issue?" is a typical statement in this mode. Passive behavior is a notch over the line.

Note that the employee also operates somewhere on the fight and flight continuum, and has the same tendency to lean in one direction or the other (Figure 14.2).

You can see I've combined the two previous figures and connected the points representing productive behavior and created a "square" or window (Figure 14.3). Problem solving cannot occur outside this window. Let's examine the four possible variations.

QUADRANT I

For example, suppose I, the manager, begin the performance appraisal in the fight mode, well outside the window of effectiveness. I'm not being merely assertive, I'm not merely presenting information or making suggestions. Right at the outset, I'm *demanding*, I'm *insisting*. "I want that budget report on my desk on the first of every month—period!"

The employee is also in the fight mode, perhaps in response to my behavior. So they say, "Hell no, I'm not doing that. Who are you to tell me what to do?"

How do I, the manager, feel during this interaction? How am I reacting to the response I'm getting? It makes me even more annoyed. How is the employee feeling during this interaction? Threatened, pushed. Does the employee feel that their manager understands them, is really interested in helping them? Not likely. How likely is it that we're resolving the problem at hand? Not likely.

QUADRANT II

I, the manager, am still in the fight mode: "This is what I want you to do and I expect you to do it!"

The employee, being eager to escape the situation and avoid confrontation, says, more or less, "Yes sir, and how high do you want me to jump?"

How do I feel during this action? Powerful. "Hey, what a boss I am. Do I know how to manage people!" But a couple weeks or months later, when nothing has changed in the employee's performance, I might realize what had happened—my employee only agreed with me to avoid a confrontation right there in my office. His reaction didn't translate into any long-term commitment. I didn't make any progress with that employee.

In fact, I fell back a few steps. After giving in without real agreement, the employee feels defeated and anticipates the future with dread. Perhaps he'll get his revenge with "passive-aggressive" behavior, quietly undermining my efforts in the future. His concerns have not been addressed; he hasn't had his say. Perhaps I've planted the seeds of a long-term worry about this job. Whatever the feelings produced by a grilling from me, they probably won't result in eager cooperation with my plans.

QUADRANT III

I, the manager, am in the flight mode. It's not easy to present an idea in this frame of mind, but I try. Here's how I phrase it: "You know, I was just wondering, is it conceivable that you might consider the possibility of thinking about perhaps doing this?" Ralph, in the fight mode, says, "That's a ridiculous suggestion. No way, I'm not doing that, forget it." I say, "Uh—OK (gulp) just though I'd ask."

How would I, the manager, feel under such circumstances? I think "ineffectual" covers it. How about the employee? "What a manager I got! I got a manager that's really understanding." We're not doing a lot of problem solving here.

QUADRANT IV

Finally, what if *both* of us, manager and employee, are in the flight mode? It's not impossible: in fact the scenario might sound familiar to you. What's our exchange going to be like? We might not even have a meeting, but supposing we're forced to get together, I might begin with, "Well, Veronica, how are things going this year?" She says, "Great!" I say, "Well, OK. Another performance appraisal taken care of. See you next year." No problems solved.

These extremes are for illustrative purposes and may seem pretty obvious. But the basic point is that when either the manager or the employee are outside the parameters of this window, problem solving cannot happen. Therefore I should not attempt a rational discussion under those circumstances. Instead I need to recognize defensiveness when it occurs, and then, once I've identified it, intervene to defuse it before proceeding with the discussion.

Imagine that this window is in front of you during the performance appraisal. You are moving through the appraisal, monitoring your own emotional level as well as the employee's. Everything's going fine until you get to one particular question, and now the other party gets defensive; or you get a little tense because of the reply. This issue must be dealt with before you can proceed further.

MANAGERS MANAGING
THEIR OWN RESPONSE

It's important to remember that there are two sides to dealing with defensiveness in any interaction. One is managing the employee's behavior, which we will discuss in more detail in a moment, but first managers must manage their own behavior.

For example, let's suppose during the performance appraisal discussion I say, "Well, based upon my review of the data I feel that this is the action we should take to resolve the problem."

A good start. Reasonable—but I'm presenting my point of view. By way of reply to that polite, reasonable statement, my employee says something like, "Who are you to tell me what to do? You're not there every day, you don't want to live with the reality of that approach. That's a ridiculous solution and I'm not doing it."

What's my natural response to those remarks if I were to allow it to drive me into defensiveness? If my natural inclination is to the fight mode, I might say, with an edge in my voice, "Who do you think you're talking to?"

I hope it's clear by now that however "natural" such a reply might be, it would be a step in the wrong direction if your intention is to defuse the situation and eventually gain the employee's cooperation.

To be in a better position to monitor myself, I'd try and identify my own natural style. Whatever that style is, my position as a manager probably requires that I move in the direction of "assertive" when I'm with my employees: that's inevitable because I have to take an active role with them; I have to present information or make suggestions. This is probably easy to maintain when no threat is present.

To find out what your natural style is, think of your behavior in your personal life. If you have children, you might watch how you behave with them. Suppose you make a reasonable suggestion to one of your children and the child looks up and says, "No!" How do you respond then? Do you say, "Oh, well, John, let me explain to you why I think it might be a good idea for you to do it this way." Or do you give up in frustrations after a few attempts to do it?

Or do you evoke the perennial, "Just who do you think is the parent here?"

Whatever it is, that's you, that's your natural style, and that's what you may have to modify consciously if you want a more productive discussion.

Or how do you react when your husband or wife or mother clams up and refuses to talk to you? For most of us it's easier to deal with someone who is overtly angry—we can talk it through with them and maybe after a while they calm down. But it's harder to know what to do if the person doesn't talk to you for three days and every time you say, "What's wrong, dear," the other person says, "Nothing!" Observe how you react, because you might encounter flight mode behavior in an employee during the performance appraisal discussion. For example, is your tendency to raise your voice? To express exasperation? You might try to get some feedback from friends and relatives. If you do tend to raise your voice, and are now aware of that tendency, you might then simply monitor yourself and consciously drop the volume of your voice when dealing with an employee who clams up during the performance appraisal discussion. It will make you more effective in that situation; it will keep you from adding fuel to the fire. This is not a hard concept to grasp. It is just a matter of awareness and acting in your best interest now that you are aware.

MANAGING THE EMPLOYEE'S RESPONSE

While monitoring myself, I may also need to monitor the employee. I may encounter defensive behavior at any point during the appraisal. I may be involved in the creation of a development plan and may be at the performance plan portion of the appraisal. Before I can take action you have to realize that the employee has passed out of the parameters of the window of effectiveness. How do I recognize defensive behavior?

How to Recognize Defensiveness

Defensiveness can be obvious or it can be subtle. It might be that the employee is continually changing the subject. I might not notice it at first, but I find myself thinking, "Wait a minute, how did we get on this topic?" The conversation is drifting, and only gradually do I begin to suspect why. I might, at that point, wait and watch for a way to make sure that's what's really happening. Now that I'm watching it, it's obvious—I ask a question, and the employee answers some other question. I say to myself, "I don't think we're in a productive mode here, I'd better do something."

The employee is starting to talk faster, scowling, or seems calm in most respects, but is tapping his or her pencil or showing some other sign of agitation.

I will not attempt to give an exhaustive list of all the non-verbal signals of defensiveness. There's no need to, because recognizing them is a skill we use in ordinary life. In your personal life you've learned to recognize tell tales signs of anger or stress in people near to you: they're tapping their foot, or their foot is going in a circle while they're watching TV. You learn to think: "Dinner's not going to go too smoothly tonight." You recognize those signs automatically with people you know well. With your employees, however, you are on less intimate terms, so you have to make more of an effort to be actively conscious of these signs.

Employee is Overly Quick to Agree

Sometimes employees start off by raising their voice but they can't sustain the aggressive mode. They growl, then they get kind of flustered, and quickly say "OK, I guess you're right." Some managers think that this means the problem is resolved; that's an error. It's true that the employee is no longer behaving aggressively, but they haven't stopped in the window of effectiveness. They've jumped all the way to the other side, which is ultimately just as unproductive as if they were ranting and raving and shaking their head no. You want them to be able to think clearly, engage in problem solving and make agreements to which they can stick.

Once managers see any of these tell-tale signs of defensive behavior, they can take steps to defuse them. The techniques that I'm about to suggest may seem very simple and basic to you; I hope they do, because then you should have no trouble applying them. The trouble is that managers *forget* to apply them, or don't think to apply them, because they are themselves under stress. Finally, they are deceptively simple.

Remember, flight and fight are primitive emotions which reside to a strong degree in all of us. I used to train police officers in family crisis intervention, which is, by the way, where 80 percent of the injury to police officers occurs. One day they may be called to the scene of a domestic dispute in a forbidding neighborhood, there's lots of trash on the street; not the kind of street where you would walk in the evening without looking behind you. When they arrive they each stand on either side of the door, tap on the door with their night stick, and announce, "Police." They're on guard, ready to deal with whatever's inside.

The next day they may get a domestic dispute call in a nice suburban area. The grass is nicely trimmed, the trees are well-kept; there are cute little ceramic knick-knacks on the lawn. The police officers are calmly talking to each other as they knock on the door on which there's a plaque that says "Dr. So & So." The door opens, and there's Dr. So and So holding a shotgun.

The point is that emotions are primitive and when people are upset they're not going to respond intellectually. There are only two categories of response possible, but of course a range of responses within each category. Cognitive logical deduction is not, however, included.

The steps here are simple but I urge you to try them. When the front desk staff of a hotel is trained in how to deal tactfully with irate guests, these steps are the core procedures; and they're also the steps counselors advise we take when dealing with children and spouses; they're basic good communication skills applied to this one special problem—what to do when confronted by another person's defensiveness.

1. Allow it
2. Restate their position
3. Acknowledge their feelings
4. Pause to allow your acceptance to sink in
5. Ask for more information on their point of view

Allow It. First of all, what do I mean by "Allow it?" In our society we have a tendency not to permit people to be upset. In supermarkets little children making a commotion are told by their parents, "Little Johnny, be a man—be quiet." "You're a big boy now, you're too old to cry."

In other words, we equate maturity with control of the emotions, and when someone loses control in our presence we tend to become embarrassed, cough, look the other way: "Well, we don't have to discuss this now. I didn't mean for it to be a big deal. Let's forget about it. We'll talk about it tomorrow."

We don't allow the person to be upset because it makes us upset. If Robert is upset, even though you don't agree with the reason, or you wouldn't have gotten upset in his place, you should allow it. The fact that he's upset is not a problem in itself. The alternative is to ignore or try to stifle the emotion. This only results in it smoldering below the surface. Even though the subject is changed, Robert is still upset. Now it interferes with everything else. Don't allow the mere fact that the employee is upset lead you to push it away.

The next steps occur in quick succession.

Restate Their Position. Remember restatement as one of the types of comments we spoke about under listening skills? This is the same technique. And in this instance you *acknowledge their feelings*, then you *pause* for a second and then *ask for more information on their point of view*.

Here's how it might sound. Robert is upset. I say "Well, Robert, I guess based on the information you have, you feel that I've taken into account issues which are extraneous, and therefore the overall rating is unfair. Based upon that you feel not only disappointed but perhaps even a little angry at me for not having mentioned that those were the important issues." (I pause for three seconds.) "What made you think that . . ." and I ask another question to draw them out a little bit more.

You may wonder what makes that pause important enough to list it above as a separate step in the process. To explain it, let me use an example from your personal life. This time *you're* mad, and the person you're mad at says to you, "Oh, I didn't realize that that bothered you. If I had known that that would annoy you I certainly would never have done it. I'm certainly glad you spoke up about it. I could have done it again and I wouldn't have realized. I'll be very careful next time. By the way, what's for dinner?"

"By the way what's for dinner?" tagged on the end without a pause suggests that the issue has been dismissed. A pause serves a very valuable purpose. It gives the person the sense that you're soaking it in. You're accepting it and taking it into account. "Okay I'll be more careful; I didn't realize it upset you so much." A pause. *Then,* "By the way what's for dinner."

In the context of the performance appraisal discussion, the pause lets them know that you're taking their objection seriously.

Try this sequence of events. It takes only a few seconds. I can't guarantee that every time someone gets upset, this procedure will resolve it, but it will help over the long run, in most cases with most people.

Overtly expressed defensiveness occurs fairly frequently. But what does a manager do about an employee who, right in the middle of this discussion, starts giving the silent treatment? Asking questions and expressing wonderment or curiosity may be very effective in cases like that. "Well, I guess from your reaction, Robert, that you must not think that it's appropriate, fair or reasonable—you haven't said how you felt—I'm kind of guessing at it. But I am kind of curious, why did you approach it that way?" Or "I wouldn't have thought though that you would have approached it that particular way. I'm kind of curious as to why you did." Express curiosity and ask more questions; even guessing at employees positions might not be a bad idea. And then they might correct you. "Oh, well, no, It's not that I'm—I'm not really—I'm not really offended, it's just that . . ." and they start talking. That's the goal.

Steps Toward Problem Solving

Once a manager has raised the important issue and has defused the employee's defensiveness, he or she is ready to engage in problem solving. Here are some steps that have been found useful in winning an employee's cooperation.

1. Define the problem (get agreement)
2. Analyze the problem
3. Consider possible solutions
4. Examine and select a solution
5. Implement and follow up

Define the Problem. It's critical for the manager to make sure that the employee agrees there *is* a problem and what that problem is. The manager may be surprised by what is said: "Well, it's true, the reports are not handed in on time on a regular basis. So what? It doesn't matter."

If it *does* matter, it should be talked through: "Well, what do you think will happen if this continues?" Once the employee is aware that there's a problem and it has consequences, the manager has to make that the employee understands that he or she is *an agent in the problem*. A manager can't proceed to the next step until the employee realizes this.

Analyze the Problem. With the employee, as manager I'd want to explore the ramifications of the problem. This is quite important: out of discussion will come the possible solutions. "Well what are the factors that caused this to happen? What other areas does it affect? What are all the dynamics?" I want the employee to think the problem through with me, so we'll both understand all its implications.

Consider Possible Solutions. Of course I've probably decided already what needs to be done. So I could say, "Well based upon this analysis of the problem, let's apply this solution." But that doesn't work as well when I want the other person to implement the solution.

The need to get a lot of options on the table in order to persuade the employee that *this* is the solution. I might say, "Go do this, Howard." But if I don't, for example, give Howard the opportunity to think the problem through he might not buy into my solution, might not do it with the dispatch or intensity or clarity that I'd like. So I need to get a lot of solutions on the table. And if in fact Howard really evolves a solution of his own that he's willing to do, that he's feels excited about and interested in—it might not be a bad idea to let him go ahead with that solution. It takes a little longer than my solution; it might not be the way I'd deal with the problem, but it'll work.

Or, as I cover the various options, he may get to the point where he says, "I hate the idea, but I guess I have to do it this way. All the other options are really not as efficient." By taking him through the various possibilities, one at a time, I've brought him to the point where he can commit himself to my solution.

Implement and Follow Up. I can't implement and follow up during the actual discussion; but I can and should discuss methods of implementation and suggest a specific follow up plan to see how the solution is working, complete with qualifying dates and targets and milestones. My employees will know that I am committed to solving this problem, which will in turn cement their own commitment to solving it.

CHAPTER FIFTEEN

Conducting Fair and Legal Performance Appraisals

Some managers are put off by the Equal Employment Opportunity Commission rules. They don't like feeling accountable to another authority, beyond their superiors in their own organization, for the way they conduct the performance appraisal; they can't help wondering whether they might be tripped up by technicalities of the law even when their judgments are fair and accurate; and in general they regard the regulations as an extra burden on an already difficult job.

I could produce many arguments in response to these complaints. For example, I could point out that while most of us may be fair enough on our own initiative without any governmental prodding, unfortunately everyone isn't like that: therefore the regulations are necessary. Then, it's really unavoidable that a procedure which has important consequences for decisions about salary and career path should occasionally be subjected to legal scrutiny:

most of us would want to have some recourse if we felt we were unfairly treated in these matters.

I could add that EEOC guidelines don't ask us to do anything we shouldn't be doing as part of our job as managers. The key criteria of the guidelines are the same as the key performance appraisal criteria presented in this book: job relevance, accuracy, documentation. In fact, the rules for fairness are identical to the rules for good business practice.

The pros and cons these issues raise could fill hundreds of pages, but they are part of a debate that is really outside the scope of this book. For our purposes, it's enough to note that whatever we may think of them, EEOC regulations are a reality. Fortunately, they're not as burdensome a reality as some believe. As we'll see, the best protection is to conduct accurate performance reviews, based on good documentation.

There are five major fair employment laws which affect the appraisal process:

1. Title VII of the Civil Rights Act—This act stipulates that an employer may not discriminate against an employee in hiring and promotion practices because of the individual's race, color, sex, creed or national origin.
2. The Equal Pay Act—This act says that employees who perform similar jobs must be paid equally.
3. The Age Discrimination in Employment Act—This act was designed to protect employees and applicants more than 40 years old. It states that employers may not discriminate against individuals in this age group in their hiring and promotion practices.
4. Section 503 of the Rehabilitation Act—This law forbids discrimination in hiring and promotion of the handicapped.
5. The Vietnam Era Veterans' Readjustment As-

sistance Act—Requires companies with government contracts of $10,000 or more to take affirmative action to employ and advance in employment qualified disabled veterans and veterans of the Vietnam era.

In 1978, to clarify the exact requirements that performance appraisal systems must meet, the Equal Employment Opportunity Commission (EEOC) published the Uniform Guidelines on Employee Selection procedures, which included the following:

1. The organization must demonstrate that the process is "valid," that is, job-related, and that it accurately measures significant aspects of job performance.
2. The organization must demonstrate that the appraisal system is the best available method, that no other system is less discriminatory.

A manager should be aware of these laws and their provisions throughout the appraisal process. In general, the burden of the proof that the appraisal system which the organization uses is fair and legal rests with the organization. Few organizations have attempted to "validate" their systems. At the same time, all organizations are subject to a periodic audit by the EEOC or other agencies. If the company's appraisal practices are not in compliance with these laws, the organization may be fined or become involved in time consuming and costly lawsuits. Individual complaints may mushroom to class action suits if the investigating agency finds evidence that the appraisal practices are not fair or equitably handled.

Knowing the laws and how to avoid violating them in the appraisal process can save an organization time and money; it can generate goodwill with individuals and create a positive public image.

TECHNIQUES FOR ENSURING
FAIR AND LEGAL APPRAISALS

In addition to knowing the law and possibly your own organization's affirmative action plan, if there is one, it is important that you develop a sensitivity to the overall goals of the EEOC guidelines. You should make an effort to avoid stereotypical ideas— and avoid using stereotypical terms—with regard to women, minorities, veterans, older workers or other "protected" groups.

In addition, managers should take the following specific steps:

1. Understand the performance factors and make sure that they and the performance objectives you generate with the employee are based on realistic expectations. The objectives should be developed to reflect actual needs of the job. The questions and issues you delve into during the discussions which center around the performance appraisal should be restricted to those areas. Having developed legitimate objectives and keeping the discussion focused on them will help ensure a fair and legal appraisal.
2. Maintain positive rapport during your discussions with the employee. Not only is this necessary in order to meet your other managerial objectives, it also helps avoid unnecessary complaints of unfairness and, perhaps, charges of discrimination from employees who received an appraisal which surprised them.
3. Do not enter into discussions which focus on qualities or attributes of the person based on their membership in any of the protected groups. If employees refer to their membership, it is best for you not to respond. For example, suppose Jack, who is 60, says, "At my age it gets harder

to see the small details. I guess that explains my trouble with this." It would be appropriate for you to focus on how to insure Jack is able to see well enough to perform his job. It would be an error for you to make any mention of his age, either to him or anyone else, or certainly not on the written part of his appraisal, even though he brought the subject up.

4. Eliminate or rephrase questions and comments that are not necessary to help you assess the employee's performance. For example, in a discussion with a female employee who had been late on a number of occasions, it is not important from a practical standpoint for you to ask about child care—nor, in fact, would it be legal. Your role is to inform her of the requirements of the job and to gain a commitment from her that she will be more punctual. Even if you have some useful suggestions regarding child care, the best assistance you can give is to direct her to someone who is not responsible for her appraisal.

To sum up, you can get all the information you need and state all of your expectations related to the job. You may not make any reference to the illegal topics relating to the "protected" groups of the Equal Employment Opportunity Commission. The best way of protecting yourself from entering into those areas is to stick to the actual job requirements and your realistic expectations of performance.

Index

The italicized page numbers indicate the locations of Figure illustrations and captions.